*Disclaimer: The information pre					and
does not constitute health or med					ok
is for informational purposes onl					se,
treat, cure, or prevent any conditio*

# Table of Contents

CHAPTER 1 Hello! .................................................................... 2

CHAPTER 2 Another Before Story ...................................... 14

CHAPTER 3 A New Life ...................................................... 20

CHAPTER 4 It's not the flu ................................................... 24

CHAPTER 5 Bad Times Galore ............................................ 26

CHAPTER 6 Personal Preference Power ............................. 35

CHAPTER 7: Drinking Momentum? Or Non-Drinking Momentum? . 38

CHAPTER 8 Shut Up, Alcohol! ........................................... 43

CHAPTER 9 The Opposite Game ........................................ 50

CHAPTER 10 Let's get shouty ............................................. 60

CHAPTER 11 Filtering ........................................................ 65

CHAPTER 12 The myth of perfection ................................. 73

CHAPTER 13 That tool you hate ......................................... 77

CHAPTER 14 No thanks, I'm not drinking ......................... 82

CHAPTER 15 The other tool you hate ................................ 90

CHAPTER 16 Finances ....................................................... 94

CHAPTER 17 Certainty ....................................................................... 98

CHAPTER 18 Creativity ..................................................................... 102

CHAPTER 19 Why it's not about how much we drink ...................... 106

CHAPTER 20 Controlling Alcohol ..................................................... 109

CHAPTER 21 Biscuits ........................................................................ 119

CHAPTER 22 Before you go… ......................................................... 122

To my Clarkey. Thank you for being my five.
I love you, all the time.

# CHAPTER 1

# Hello!

Hi. Welcome to **Shut Up, Alcohol!**

This little book you hold in your hands took a decade of procrastination to finish, so I'm very pleased your eyeballs have made their merry way here.

If we haven't met yet, then allow me to introduce myself. I'm Carrie Carlisle, and **Shut Up, Alcohol!** is a self-support method that I invented many moons ago, to take charge of our drinking, today.

This book was written to explain how and why I use my method, and to show you how you can, too.

It's not massively long, the method itself is very simple. But the results are massive. I speak with personal experience of this.

Since inventing and consistently using **Shut Up, Alcohol!** from 2006 onwards, I have been utterly transformed on every single level imaginable.

Obviously the most important result, is that I am no longer a drinker. And I was a drinker. A heavy one, at that. My drinking was an absolute default setting:

Happy? Drink.

Upset? Drink.

Angry? Drink.

Bored? Drink. Etc.

I drank in response to everything. Including all the (self-made) chaos that seemed to constantly surround me.

I lost jobs, friendships, relationships. My health (physical and mental.) You name it, I used alcohol to destroy it. For years.

**But that was then.**

Now I am utterly indifferent to alcohol. I don't care about it. It never crosses my mind. I never notice alcohol, or who is still drinking it.

Not only that. I feel like I've always been a non-drinker.

So that's a bit of a result.

The only struggle for me is connecting with my old-drinking self. It takes a lot of effort because I think, look, and act nothing like her. Which I guess explains why this book took ten years to write, eh...

Am I a temple of self-discipline? Good grief, no.

In fact, I have zero willpower, either.

Full disclosure: I am married to a former athlete.

If ever there was any doubt that I am the polar opposite of self-mastery and control? Then watching Mr C's natural-born competitive approach to absolutely everything in life, has well and truly sorted that out.

I mean, the man switches the kettle on to make his morning coffee, *then races himself* to empty the dishwasher before that kettle boils.

Every. Single. Morning.

Therefore, if stopping drinking had been an Olympic Sport? There would have been no gold medal for me.

(This is a terrible analogy. Mainly because he was a footballer, not an Olympian, let's swiftly move on, shall we?)

The point is, I'm indifferent to alcohol, effortlessly. So, I know you can be, too.

The most important thing to know about my method, **Shut up, Alcohol!** Is that, although it's very simple to learn and use, it has a rigidly solid framework, with explicit instructions. Explained one-by-one.

And that really matters. This is the biggest reason for its success, actually.

**Because I truly believe that it is vague advice and wishy-washy tips, that make our drinking habits so hard to change, not alcohol itself.**

When I was drinking heavily and actually wanted to stop, (took a while to get there, mind you). I found that so-called help, came in the following categories:

- Dry statistics from qualified medics with no personal understanding or empathy
- Sober people "white knuckling" it and insisting everyone else must do the same.
- Those who knew a successful method but wanted to make lots of money out of it, so drip-fed some of the key elements, to make people eternally dependant on them.
- Those who misappropriated other people's methods, then tried passing off a second-rate version as their own. Without the same understanding of it as the inventor.

We all have instincts. Often as heavy drinkers, we learn to turn ours off, or just dismiss them, but they are still there. We can sense when someone isn't telling us the truth, or trying to sell us a made-up story, instead of sharing their own.

The well-being industry has never been bigger. To put it bluntly: Sober Sells. Of course, people want to cash in on that. And, if they are providing a good service that genuinely helps people, then fair play to them, no judgement from me.

Sadly, not everyone is, so we must keep our wits about us.

Luckily, people rarely get rich from writing books. Especially little ones, without child wizards in them. So it's safe to say I'm not in this for the money.

Then why do it?

Information sharing. That's it. End of.

We live in an age where anyone who has a solution to a problem, can get that information to people, cheaply and easily. And that really excites me. It speaks to my values and makes my life a fulfilling experience.

Plus, I make good money, because people who are effortless light or non-drinkers, (indifferent to alcohol), make good money. It's a natural side-effect, more on that later though…

I do not rely on any part of the addiction/recovery/sobriety industries to make my living.

It's important to me that you know this, because one thing that's always made me uneasy about alcohol-free thought leaders, speakers, authors, and other professionals in this space, is that they don't seem to have a life or income outside of the addiction arena.

How can any of us claim to be of genuine service to other people, if we reside in an echo-chamber?

I'm going to put my husband and I's work website right here,

(www.clarkeandcarrie.com ) so you can see that I am a real person who has a fully rounded life.

Because having a fully rounded life is the foundation to becoming *totally and permanently, indifferent to alcohol.* Which is the number one aim of this book, and my method. Regardless of which path you choose to get there.

Anyway, where were we? Ah yes, the framework is important because: **No Manual.**

Do you ever feel like everyone else in life was handed a manual, but you never got yours? I know I do.

And it turns out, there's a good reason for that…

I'm not a self-starter, never have been. And there are loads of life tasks, some simple, others more complicated, that I never learned how to do.

If you feel that way too, it might be worth considering the following:

Most of us try alcohol for the first time as young teenagers, some grow out of it super quickly, others slightly later, let's say during or after Uni.

Of those who are still drinking a lot in their twenties, maybe settling down in their first serious relationship, changes their alcohol consumption.

Others stay single but really enjoy their career, and they gradually embrace a work routine that has no room for binge drinking, so it fades into the background. Many decide that having kids and a hangover isn't doable, so that's their natural stopping point,

Let's go back to the people who ducked out of drinking as teenagers. Perhaps they didn't like the taste, had alcoholic relatives, whatever, either way, it wasn't for them.

The point is these individuals had their entire formative years to learn skills and pay attention to the world around them. Developing strong personal preferences, and generally become competent humans.

The folk that stopped drinking as young adults, maybe in Uni or starting their first jobs? Sure, they are a bit behind the sensible teenagers, so don't know quite as much as them, and will lag a little. But they show up to life early enough to learn a lot about the outside world, and to form their own inner identity.

And so, on it goes, with each little subgroup.

Until you get way down the bottom, to the heavy drinkers.

We who never learned our true inner selves because we arrested development at the age we started drinking.

Who didn't form strong personal preferences. Or develop basic life skills that other functional adults take for granted.

I may have stopped drinking and become indifferent to alcohol since 2006, but I'm still catching up with the life manual.

Not that it matters now, because as soon as I realised why, I was able to adapt accordingly.

For me that means saying *shut up and take my money*, to anyone who has built a solid framework that shows me, step-by-step, how to master a skill I know I lack.

Some of this is personal development based, therapists and coaches.

But a lot are practical. Driving lessons. DIY. Being organised. Learning new hobbies. How to cook. How to pay bills on time, even

Basically, there's not a lot I ever try and tackle by myself, for the first time. It just takes far too long. Because: **No Manual**. I've accepted that I started too late to organically develop my own. So, I pay other people who are very good in their specific field, to help me learn what I can.

**All heavy drinkers struggle without solid framework. It's a natural consequence of our drinking.**

**Yet, for decades now, we have all been given only the vaguest guidance on how to stop drinking, or control alcohol. And absolutely no solid framework.**

**Only to be told the reason we can't change, is because alcohol is powerful, and addiction is mysterious!**

How absolutely ridiculous is that??

Alright, rant over, let's crack on. I want to talk to you about who the **Shut Up, Alcohol!** method, is for.

I'll be honest, I only invented it to stop myself drinking. It works, obviously, so that was it, as far as I was concerned, job done. I never in a million years thought about teaching this technique to other people.

I didn't even talk about being a non-drinker, who is indifferent to alcohol, for the first seven years of my stopping drinking.

(Stay tuned, more on that later.)

When I was finally satisfied, that I knew what I was talking about, I did indeed start sharing my own unique perspective on non-drinking.

I would do little podcasts or interviews for people who ran "sober businesses", for want of a better phrase. I was working as a TV Presenter when I first started discussing my journey, and I had a blog as well as writing for different online newspapers, so my stuff was quite widely read.

I would talk on the radio and television, usually reaction pieces, or just any time producers needed a talking head for alcohol or addiction discussions.

And women contacted me, from all over the shop! Some were a lot like me. Others were from places in the world I had never even been to.

Lots had jobs that were nothing like mine. I was single and childless at the time. Yet loads of the women getting in touch with me for my help, were wives and mothers.

I had never worked in the corporate space. Yet still, high-powered career women were resonating with my way of doing things. And they would ask me to show them the method I had taught myself. So, after a lot of persuasion, I did. (Throughout this book, I will refer to sessions of teaching other women my method. So, just to add context, back in the day, I used to do one-to-one virtual sessions, via Skype. This was years before working-from-home, or Zoom meetings, were a thing. I don't teach one-to-one sessions nowadays. But you have this book, instead. So, happy days!

There were three sessions, one session per week. This was more than enough time to teach the method, let the person go off and practice it, and then answer any subsequent questions that arose. There was always email support afterwards, if needed, and an occasional refresher session for long term maintenance. But the idea has always been to get people going on their own, not to manipulate people into becoming repeat customers.)

It didn't matter how alike, or how different we were. I taught them how I had stopped drinking, *with the emphasis on being indifferent to alcohol*, then they copied me and got the exact same results.

Except one lady.

Don't get me wrong, she made flying progress at first, just as I would expect.

We did the first two sessions, but she kept cancelling the third.

Weeks later, I managed to pin her down for the final one.

She was monosyllabic. Very withdrawn. Not the feisty, funny, forthright woman I had gotten to know in our previous sessions, not at all.

Then she burst into tears.

Now, tears are totally normal when it comes to confiding in someone else that our drinking is out of control. All this stuff we hide from other people. It's scary to let it out, even in front of someone like me, who has been there and done it all, too.

But these weren't those sort of tears.

She kept saying over and over again *"I've failed, I'm useless, I can't do this properly, there's no point."* Again, all words I've heard before, but only ever in the first session, before we start.

Or, if someone stops following the **Shut Up, Alcohol!** method, by trying to complicate it, unnecessarily.

I asked her what she meant, and she admitted that she had been away for work, (she's a mega successful CEO) and had started drinking.

It didn't add up to me at all, she gave no binge-drinking vibes (I know them well, obviously) so I enquired how bad the episode had been.

She told me she had two drinks, every night, for a three-day trip.

This was the behaviour she was currently having a breakdown over. A woman who, until recently, had secretly been regularly hospitalised by drinking accidents. Who wanted my help only a few short weeks ago because her nightly binge drinking was destroying her marriage. Who was deathly afraid of losing her career, as well as her spouse.

Now, seemingly quite able to control the amount she was drinking. I was astonished to say the least.

Not only because she was effortlessly using my method for a purpose it was never designed for. But also because she was so unhappy with the amazing results.

Though I couldn't blame her. Let's face it, there's a massive amount of animosity in recovery circles, aimed at those who aren't 100% teetotal.

It's why so many people lie and pretend to be fully sober. Which only compounds the feelings of self-loathing and fraudulence, that lead straight back to the bottle…

This lady had a very powerful belief, that she could not be successful at networking if she was teetotal at events and conferences.

*It's not true. No personal belief or value is ever fact. Merely opinion.*

Could she have rid herself of this limiting belief? Yes! Very easily. But it was her biggest stumbling block, so she decided not to at this time. And, instead of derailing completely into her old, destructive drinking patterns, she decided to use my method, with her own twist, until her limiting beliefs evolved into more helpful and supportive ones.

Basically, she wanted to give herself a new stringent framework, within my own original framework.

Because: **No Manual**, remember?

To say I was uncomfortable with this was an understatement, but at least she wasn't drinking like she used to, so fair play to her, it was a roaring success. An anomaly I would surely never see again, right?

**Except I did see it again, bloody loads of times. Once you know what you are looking for in people, everything becomes visible.**

Whilst up until this point, the overwhelming majority of people took my **Shut Up, Alcohol!** method and quite happily became authentic non-drinkers, like myself. There were also those who chose to let a small amount of alcohol into their lives, because, after a lot of safe exploration, it felt more authentically like they were light drinkers.

And I do mean *far smaller amounts* than previously. Closely monitored. But guess what, they also saw great success doing that!

If they could get past the bit where they could honestly admit that this was what they were doing, and transparently owning their deliberate behaviour. Instead of trying to appear "perfect", that is.

It's not something I would ever have chosen to teach, off my own back. I was all about that sober life!

But, like anything we choose to share, my method quickly became bigger than me, and my own ideals. Even within the very small circles I was teaching it in.

I had to let my ego take a back seat and use this new information to serve as many women as possible. *Because being of service is what information sharing is all about, in the end.*

**The overwhelming majority of this book is about building a solid foundation of real, authentic disinterest and indifference to alcohol.**

**Regardless of whether we intend to be 100% alcohol-free, or not.**

By default I will generally refer to non-drinking/alcohol-free behaviour. Firstly, because that's how I live.

But secondly, because there is not a huge difference in the feeling place, between the actions of light drinking, or being teetotal, when both are done from a mindset of indifferent effortlessness. It's just not a big deal.

(Okay, fine. I get it. This is controversial stuff. And can I just say that it absolutely *was* a big deal in my mind too, for years, without me even thinking to question it. Until I finally bit the bullet and started drinking again for this book. Then stopped, effortlessly, more on that later.)

The contrast is only evident when we decide to forgo making our subconscious mind our friend. Genuinely tackling unhelpful beliefs that do not serve us. Making alcohol the boss because we don't want the hassle of being in charge.

Once all of the exercises are familiar to you, and your brain has adjusted to using them, it is up to you to decide what your true relationship with alcohol is. The situation that brings you the most peace, and affords you the most headspace.

(Ps I hate the phrase "alcohol-free". Makes me feel like a beverage, rather than a human. Why are all sober-type phrases so dreadful?)

This rock-solid foundation is why the women who choose to use **Shut Up Alcohol!** to drink controlled amounts, can actually do so.

***Because they fully learned the non-drinking bits of the method, first.***

So please don't just skip to the "controlling alcohol" chapter and expect success. It's all been assembled, in the right order for very deliberate reasons.

The absolute bare minimum you should expect from this book, is to change your relationship with alcohol in two hours.

To grasp the basics of the exercises, so you can start and incorporate them into your day-to-day life, permanently.

**And- most importantly- understand why it's been so hard to try and control or stop drinking in the past. So, you can finally stop doing the very things that have been unwittingly making this**

**process so difficult**.

So that you can become genuinely indifferent to alcohol.

Bare. Minimum.

How far you take your new easy life beyond that, is totally up to you… Something to bear in mind whilst reading this book, is that I talk about teaching women this method, directly. But about people in general, reading the book and doing the exercises.

This is because, although men used to comment on my articles, and actually get amazingly fast results, using the brief tips I gave in them. Only women ever contacted me for one-to-one sessions, so it is women's experiences I draw on in this book.

I do believe this method works for everyone, irrespective of their gender.

One more thing I will mention, is how short this book is. I've deliberately kept it as brief as humanly possible, mainly because where alcohol abounds, concentration never resides.

Also, I may be a non-drinker, but I have the concentration span of a drunken newt. I would never finish a self-help book that took longer to read, than a film would take to watch, so I don't expect you to, either.

I'm confident that the quality of the tools in Shut Up, Alcohol! negates any pointless drawing out of eloquent theories. I hope you feel that way by the end, too. I get in there with a tool, give an example on how to use it, and then leave. Because that's how simple the concepts are. I'd rather you started incorporating them straight away, than be bogged down by endless hypotheticals.

# CHAPTER 2

# Another Before Story

Not gonna lie, I'd rather swallow my own face than write this part of the book. But needs must.

I used to love reading people's before and after stories, in what is nowadays called "Quit Lit" genre.

It was my absolute favourite hangover activity when I was struggling to ditch the booze, back in my willpower days.

Well maybe second favourite, do panic attacks count as a favourite hangover activity? Or maybe third, if vomiting and self-loathing are also contenders.

Ah yes, good old before and afters. The horror stories of before, followed by the almighty testaments to sober salvation that were always the after.

So inspirational. So unrelatable. So not happening for me.

My before is already documented heavily, to be honest. I was in "A Royal Hangover", documentary. Then there were blogs, newspapers, tv broadcasts, you name it, I've shared it. So, I'm not going to repeat a lot of it. Just the important bits.

Well, I say important, but my own before story is pretty much the same as everyone else's I have ever read.

It's the during and after parts where it all gets a bit…well…weird…

I started drinking at 15 years old. I was always a good girl up to that point, so the immediate grip alcohol had on me was a total shock. But it was instant. I felt like I had found the solution to all my problems. Like a lovely big duvet had been wrapped around me. All the social awkwardness and self-consciousness I had felt as a teenager? Instantly gone. What a result!

Until I was sick and passed out, obviously.

From then on, drinking was my favourite and only hobby. I was always keen to start. And never knew when-or how- to stop.

I drank heavily through the rest of school, and then ramped it up a gear in Uni. Fortunately for me I am from Newcastle, a city in the North East of England that was, at the time, known as the "Binge Drinking Capital of Europe". So, my dysfunctional relationship with alcohol, whilst still on the higher end of acceptable, was still culturally appropriate.

Throughout this time, even at such a young age, there were warning signs. A huge one, when I was 19, that I'm still amazed didn't bring up any red flags for myself, or the medical professionals around me.

I had slipped a disc in my back that required surgery. I was in hospital, about to be prepped for theatre, when a nurse came in to my room and said he had to take more blood, as there had been an error with my results.

An hour later the surgeon appeared and told me there would be no operation today.

My white cells were so low, that I would have been killed or paralysed, had he gone ahead, due to "unstoppable and catastrophic, bleeding."

That my white cells were so low, I could die just from hitting my head on something and so was unable to leave my hospital bed, until further notice.

And that the most likely explanation for my symptoms, was leukaemia.

Long story short, I did not have leukaemia. Turns out everyone missed the real most likely explanation for my almost non-existent white cells.

*Because, apparently, in 1999, nice young ladies like me, simply did not drink enough to destroy their own bone marrow…*

I was duly pronounced a medical anomaly, and a nice haematologist put me on prednisone. A few weeks later I underwent back surgery and, after a week-long stay in hospital, was sent on my way.

Without ever being asked a single question about my drinking habits, by the half dozen consultants involved in my care.

But the wheels really came off for me after I graduated from Uni. I definitely had a drinking problem way before then. But strict school and Uni timetables had always kept me relatively functional and safe.

Now, out in the big wide world, and with absolutely no idea what to do, I floundered.

I decided to dive head-first into a highly dysfunctional relationship with a fellow heavy drinker (no surprises there, then), and spent every day and night of the following year either drunk, hungover, or in the grips of debilitating panic attacks.

I thought moving away might help. So, I managed to win a place at a Drama

School in London and moved 300 miles away for a fresh start. The Royal Central School of Speech and Drama was old-school and posh. I was a working-class girl from Newcastle. It wasn't the best combination, to be honest.

Did it work? Did it heck! I was back to my former routine of drinking as much as my class timetables would allow. On top of that I was now living in an area with a reputation for being dangerous, that I didn't know at all.

Though I was of way more danger to myself than the area was, let's be honest. And the kindness of local strangers rescued me from bad situations I had gotten myself in, more times than I care to count.

I graduated from Drama School, (without taking them up on their frightfully helpful suggestions of elocution lessons) and guess what? Straight back to the day and night drinking. Occasionally tempered by stints of employment through the odd acting job, or temp agency gig. Yet, a lot of time it was back to the good old drink, hangover, panic attack, cycle.

My drinking was scary. I had no control over it. I sustained many injuries. Had drinks spiked. Lost jobs. Friendships. Attracted awful men. I hated my life, hated myself and could see no way of things ever changing.

Fast-forward a few years later, to me working as an actor-in-residence in a theatre in the middle of nowhere. Again, I had moved for a fresh start. Again, it hadn't worked.

As well as the panic attacks and hating my day-to-day existence, my physical health had started to suffer. This was new for me, so it got my attention.

I decided to stop drinking, using willpower. It was completely awful and, though it felt like several eternities, I actually made it to just six weeks sober.

This was actually staggeringly long for me, given the most time I had generally gone without drinking for, since the age of 18, was a couple of days.

As usual for me in every part of life, I had no game plan. I managed to scare myself sober for the first few days, but once the worrying physical symptoms had abated? Well, that didn't work for me anymore.

Instead, I would verbally beat myself up, and shame myself with examples of my past behaviour. Then I would move to counting days. Hide away in my flat, ignore the outside world. Getting as many sober days under my belt as possible, became my new fixation.

I left the house socially only once before I "broke", and that was to attend a wedding, where, as I seem to recall, the bride and groom were totally outraged at my mumbled apologies for not getting drunk with them.

Two weeks after that, I ended up in a grotty Wetherspoons pub with my mates, and that was that. My six-week run of so-called sobriety, was over.

I drank solidly for two more years after that.

In retrospect, I can see how I paved my road to "relapse" without ever meaning to. Everything about my first approach was guaranteed to fail me.

Of course, I didn't know that at the time. As far as I was concerned, this whole debacle only proved to me what a hopeless case I was.

Nevertheless, my subconscious mind must have been doing some serious overtime, trying to solve the issue of my heavy drinking, for the next couple of years. Because what came afterwards is not something I could ever have come up with through effort alone…

Fast forward again, to two years later. Its 2006 and my drinking is some of the heaviest it has ever been. It starts in the afternoon, then goes on throughout the night, almost every night.

Mornings I go to work, unless I am too hungover to function, then the whole sorry dance starts all over again.

The end is a total anti-climax, actually, as these things usually are, outside of a

Hollywood movie…

*I was sitting on the floor of yet another house party, it was the early*

*hours of the morning. And the voice in my head, the one that was usually full of nasty jibes, spoke very softly for once.*

*"If you keep living like this you are going to die."* Now, this wasn't news to me, anyone who drank as much and as regularly as I was drinking, wasn't cut out for a long, healthy life.

*No, it was my emotional reaction to this inner voice, that took me by surprise. I actually **felt something**. I was so used to feeling nothing except guilt, panic, shame, boredom, that this other emotion, came as a real shock.*

*Apparently, I didn't want to die. So that was nice.*

*I just didn't want to live like this, anymore…and maybe, just maybe…I didn't have to.*

There was a tiny modicum of hope in me at that moment. It caught me off-guard.

I decided to listen. I went home. And from that moment on, my life completely changed.

# CHAPTER 3

# A New Life

A few hours after this mini-revelation, I woke up in bed. Still drunk? Probably.

But that glimmer of hope remained, it hadn't gone away like I suspected it might.

That was enough for me to make a proper start. And I did so by inventing the first technique in the **Shut Up, Alcohol!** method.

I used the **"I Don't Know'** tool, which I will explain in a moment.

Essentially, for the first time in my whole adult life, I was honest with myself.

*And it bloody well worked.*

Like anyone who drinks at the drop of a hat, I was used to my brain thinking about drinking, whether I was hungover, currently drunk, or planning on drinking, very soon.

I refer to this as **"Drinking Momentum"** and go into further detail about it later on in a different chapter, but for now, let's just say my brain was already starting its daily obsession with drinking, versus not drinking.

But not for long.

This is how every single drinking thought was addressed, both on that day, and every single one that followed it.

Imagine! I didn't know that my first day of being a permanent non-drinker was underway! I was happy at the time, just to last the afternoon!

My Brain: *Soooo...fancy a beer then?*

Me: *No thanks Brain we can't do that anymore.*

My Brain: *Why not?*

Me: ***I Don't Know,*** *I just know that we can't.*

My Brain: *Oh, right, erm see you later.*

And I'd get a bit of peace for a few minutes...until my brain would demand a replay, or slight variation of the conversation.

My Brain: *Hiya! I see it's six o'clock and we aren't in the pub, shall we set off soon?*

Me: *Not tonight actually Brain. we can't go there.*

My Brain: *Why not?*

Me: ***I Don't Know,*** *I just know we can't, sorry.*

My Brain: *Erm, okay see you later.*

On and on it went. My mind trying desperately to play out the well-worn pattern of the heavy drinking routine, that I had adhered to for so long.

But I wasn't having it.

Something was happening. I couldn't have told you exactly what it was.

But I knew it was different, and, therefore, in the wheelie-bin fire that had become my life? Any change of behaviour could only be good.

My Brain: *Hiyaaaa Only me! Just checking to see if you've changed your mind and want to go show your face and be sociable! What do you say?*

Me: *We can't, Brain.*

My Brain: *But why not?*

Me: *I* **honestly** **Don't Know***. But I can't go to the pub and not drink. I wish I knew why. But* **I Don't Know** *why.*

Three little words. That's all. But they started me on a journey of a life transformed on every level.

A pattern of abusive drinking, halted in its tracks. And all because I was finally open and honest with myself, and my own mind didn't know how to manipulate its way around that sort of behaviour.

**Authentic truth, even at its most simplistic, will beat even the most powerful and sophisticated lie.**

In that moment, I stopped kidding myself. Never again did I try and justify my need for alcohol.

Up until this day, I had known next to nothing about emotional awareness. But now I had learned my first big lesson.

*Honesty. Always. Wins.

I didn't try and bluff my way out of the situation. I wasn't admitting I was an alcoholic. That I had a disease, or addiction and couldn't ever be cured.

I definitely had not grasped how much of a problem my drinking was, (though that became an indisputable fact, in the weeks that followed, without me ever drinking another drop of alcohol.)

Three little words that my brain could not get past, no matter what method of persuasion it used.

The push-pull had stopped, I was no longer tying myself in an emotional knot, and I was continuing to, miraculously, not drink.

Looking back, I think that may well have been enough to keep me away from alcohol, possibly forever, who knows? I wouldn't have had a beautiful and fully rounded life like I have now, but to literally stop the destructive action of drinking? Yeah, I think that would have done the trick.

If you'd asked me right then, mid 2006, what my other goals were? I would have told you there were none.

All I wanted was to be sober and perfect.

To count my days, eke out my little life, and pat myself on the back for being so brave, etc.

(We will go more into that, in the "myth of perfection" chapter later, but remember I said it, its super important.)

Now let's get to the weird part…

*If we are being totally honest with each other, then it's time I confessed to you, that in 1998, during my English Literature A Level, I picked an essay to write on 'Lost in Translation' by Brian Friel, a man of true genius,*

*Unfortunately, my penmanship and attention to detail, are not up to his exacting standards, and so I was marked down for repeatedly referring to him, as the legendary Irish playwright "Brain" Friel.*

*It's a mix-up I have never fully, psychologically recovered from, even 25 years on. Therefore,*

*I reckon there's about a 75% chance of my slipping a typo into this book, about conversations between myself and my Brian instead of me and my Brain. Sorry about that. I feel better for telling you though, already.*

# CHAPTER 4

# It's not the flu.

I can't be exact on dates here, given how it was, at this time of writing, nearly two decades ago, but at some point, before the hitting the big fortnight milestone of my sobriety. I became ill.

Really, horribly unwell. It started off feeling like the worst flu of my life.

It soon got a great deal worse.

Full body shakes, actual hallucinations of creatures climbing the walls. I saw death in the corner of the room (I mean, how completely *mortifying*, why couldn't I hallucinate something more normal for goodness' sake, something more on-trend for mid 2006, like some noughties Hollywood heart throb or new millennium pop star. I would *far rather* confess to seeing every member of NSYNC in my lavatory, than the Grim Reaper.)

I was wetting towels to help with my fever, but they kept drying and crisping up like they were on a radiator.

I knew I was in trouble; I just didn't understand what to do. So, like any good former alcohol abuser. I did nothing. Asked for no help. Decided to just wait it out.

Idiot.

The symptoms gradually abated after a few days. But I never felt right again after that.

It was alcohol withdrawal, obviously. When I realised that, it was the biggest shock of my life. How on earth could I have become physically dependent on alcohol? I didn't even drink spirits!

Well, okay I did, but only in blackout, and when no one else was around. So, it hardly counts!

Any semblance of denial about my abusive alcohol consumption came crashing down. I knew there was never any going back. The concept of truth was no longer shameful.

It was my friend. My ally. And would help me get to the next stage of my new life.

I had no idea what was coming next. Which was a blessing really. It's not something I could ever have prepared for.

My life was about to swerve completely off-track. I would never be the same again.

This is the bit where I tell you that, I get it, truly. You are used to feeling grim from loads of booze and constant hangovers. You probably also avoid doctors as much as I did, so that you don't have to tell them how much you are drinking.

But, even if, like I did, you don't think you qualify as someone who is physically dependant on alcohol.

Because you have a job/house/cat you take good care of.

Please hear me when I say that going through alcohol withdrawal alone is dangerous. If you cease drinking suddenly, and then feel very unwell within a few days *seek medical help*. Go to A&E and tell them the truth, no matter how embarrassing it feels at the time.

Hopefully it will save you going through what happened to me, next.

# CHAPTER 5

# Bad Times Galore

This bloody chapter, I swear!

I never even *talk* about any of this stuff anymore, haven't for years, hopefully never will again.

You know what? I'm not even sticking around with you for this bit, actually.

You're on your own, mate.

I'm off to eat some crisps or something.

I'll meet you at the start of the next chapter, okay? Deep breath and speed read your way through it.

Ready, steady GO!

My body never fully recovered from the ravages of alcohol withdrawal. I was fortunate that going through it didn't kill me, and, at the risk of sounding like a broken Geordie record, let me reiterate, I encourage anyone who starts to feel the way I did, after suddenly stopping heavy amounts of drinking. To get to A&E as soon as possible.

I felt weak all of the time. Every morning, after yet another 12-hour kip. I woke up feeling no rest from sleep at all. This was annoying and somewhat ironic, after years of barely sleeping, nor taking care of myself in any way.

I was now a non-drinker and had gone from smoking at least 20 cigarettes a day, to being a non-smoker, too. Yet I felt worse than when I had been drinking and smoking, day, and night.

Still, there was no question that I would go back to my old drinking habits. If anything, I now had more ammunition to fight my brain with.

My Brain: *Look at the state of you. This clearly isn't working, let's just go get pissed.*

Me: *No brain. We can't.*

My Brain: *Why not?*

Me: *I don't know why. I do know I'm never going through withdrawal again, though.*

My Brain: *Oh yeah, the Grim Reaper etc.*

Me: *EXACTLY! The Grim fecking Reaper! Mortifying! Why couldn't you have just-*

My Brain: *-for the thousandth time! I don't know why I put him there instead of Justin Timberlake, okay! I'll do better next time!*

Me: *No! it's never happening again. Shut Up, Brain!*

Then I got sick. Again.

I know, right? Seriously.

It felt as bad as withdrawal, but no hallucinations. No shakes. I didn't have a clue what was going on. This illness slammed into me. On the plus side I was unconscious for a lot of it and had actually sought medical care this time.

Spoiler Alert:

Turns out I had caught a virus that was doing the rounds. It wreaked havoc on my body, which had already been so recently destroyed by alcohol withdrawal.

In these post covid times, its accepted as normal for people to get so sick from a virus that their body is fully wrecked. But in 2006? Nope. Totally unheard of.

*So, when I lost the ability to move my arms, legs, hands, feet. When I was bedbound and unable to lift my head off my chest.* It was the most surreal experience of my life.

Every day I expected to get better. Every day it didn't happen.

Month after month went by. My parents took care of my every need. They fed, washed, and dressed me. 24 hours a day, in their spare room.

I was 26 years old.

The only step beyond that, deterioration-wise, I was warned, was being fitted with a feeding tube, if I lost the ability to swallow.

I'm thankful to this day that it did not happen.

Very, very slowly, I began to get the use of my hands back, then my arms. The day I was able to lift my own head up, was a triumph I'll never forget.

The next three years were a blur of slight physical progress, followed by small relapses.

I had lost everything. My independence. My health. I was physically, emotionally, and financially bankrupt.

If ever there a time to start drinking again, this would have been it.

Not a chance, mate.

A lot of the time I had felt helpless in this situation. But what I also felt for the first time, and actually let myself express, was *anger*.

Imagine that. I was in my late twenties by now, yet I had never expressed anger in my life.

No need when you can drink the feelings away, eh…

But now, here was anger, late to the party, but finally making its arrival.

So, when my brain decided to shoot its shot with an invitation to drink?

I was ready to stop this nonsense, once and for all.

My Brain: *Hey, so I noticed that you have absolutely nothing to live for these days...fancy a drink?*

Me: SHUT UP.

My Brain: *Erm, pardon?*

Me: SHUT UP. I am done with being pushed around. I will never drink again. Shut Up, you. And **SHUT UP ALCOHOL!**

(Turns out that all this anger I felt churning inside me, during the long years of being housebound, helpless, and hopeless. The moment I projected them onto alcohol, they evaporated. Yes, there is indeed a chapter about shouting at inanimate objects, so that's something to look forward to, eh...) And just like that, **rock solid certainty**, entered the building.

It would never depart again.

I think it's fair to say at this point that life had gotten pretty bad, and if there had ever been an excuse to drink, this situation would have been it.

But, I didn't choose that. I chose to keep going.

Because, even though I presently had less going for me, than back in my worst drinking days?

I was starting to get curious about the new me that was emerging. Although I would never have chosen the circumstances, I found myself in. Housebound. Totally reliant on other people to care for me. I also recognised it was a completely unique opportunity.

Let's face it, I had a lot of time on my hands, even if I couldn't use those hands fully.

The strange thing about being bedbound, (which I was, on and off, for years) is how completely removed you are, not just from the outside world, but from your day-to-day behaviours.

I felt like I had a Birdseye view of my own life.

I was beginning to see my old patterns of behaviour for what they truly were.

And, whilst I couldn't 100% see where this was all going, or even if I would ever get the opportunity to live any semblance of a normal life.

I recognised that the current predicament I found myself in, was also a huge opportunity for personal growth.

Up until this point, I had readily believed everything other people had told me. *Because I held so little value in my own beliefs and opinions, I was always keen to give other people's insights more weight than my own.*

Perhaps this new method I had been doing with my own brain, had opened up new possibilities for me, I don't know.

I can't say for sure what it was, but my negative gut reaction, to what medical professionals were describing as my long-term prognosis, was a first for me.

Many doctors came to see me, all bearing the same news; I shouldn't expect to get much better than I was right now. And there was every chance I could get much worse.

This was my new reality, time to accept it and get used to it.

As a drinker, I would probably have believed them. Hell, I may even have taken the opportunity to get as drunk as possible, for as long as possible, because, why not? What else was there to live for except alcohol at that point?

But this was a new me, a person that, in many ways, felt far more mentally capable than she ever had in her entire life.

To put it simply: I wasn't having any of it.

I remember thinking that I couldn't accept my independent adult life was over, at such a young age. When I had done nothing except get drunk and hate myself, for the majority of it.

What a bloody waste it had all been.

This *couldn't* be it for me, not when I had finally started to make real changes!

I chose not to believe what I was hearing, I decided to put my faith in myself.

A definite first for me.

The funny thing is, although I had absolutely nothing going for me. I had started to feel a sense of peace that I had never experienced before.

My life had been so chaotic up until that point. So full of self-perpetuating drama. That it was a relief not to be constantly harming myself like that, anymore.

I had never felt genuine peace before. Not in my entire life. It was nice, I liked it.

In a weird way, I now felt more like my true self, than I had ever done before. Despite having no job. No independence. Not a thing on the horizon to look forward to. Nothing to fill my days with. And no proof that things were likely to get any better than this.

It seemed totally illogical, yet peace became my norm.

And, as time went on (trust me when I say it dragged, on and on and on. Minutes felt like hours. Hours felt like days, etc) Yes, time went on and on and on without anything changing in my physical circumstance, but the peace remained, and with it, the realisation that, with nothing to distract me, I was finally discovering who I really was.

If this version of me truly felt more real than anything I'd ever felt in my entire adult life? And it did.

**Then it was obvious to me, that I was not supposed to be a drinker.**

That heavy drinking, was a habit I picked up, at the time. Because it papered over the cracks, it was almost a cheat code to my life.

But this inner person I was now connecting with?

*This person* felt like the real me. It was a tremendously good feeling. Powerful, nice.

I wanted more of it.

Had this version of me just been waiting in the wings for her turn, all along?

If so, as far as I was concerned, she was going to be running things, from this point on.

Because, this small belief, this inkling I had, that deep down I was authentically a non-drinker?

It was reinforced with every woman that found me, years later, down the line. *Because not a single one of us were happy, living out our lives, as drinkers.*

Not one of us felt like we were deliberately creating, or fully in charge, of an existence that really belonged to us.

Heavy drinking was just such an ingrained habit by then, that we knew simply no other way to be.

We were all looking for an out, it just so happened that mine was more dramatic than most.

*Want to hear an inconvenient truth?*

Not everyone feels the way we do.

In fact, there are lots of heavy drinkers and chronic abusers of alcohol, who feel totally at one, with their actions.

Are you outraged by that thought? Wondering what I could possibly mean by that? Think about it. I guarantee you, that you know, or know of, at least one.

I'm not saying their life is brilliant, or that the people around them benefit from their hard-drinking ways.

What I mean is, they never question their own behaviour. The thought of changing their drinking habits has never even crossed their minds.

And, whilst they drink way more than is good for them, or anyone else in their vicinity, no doubt. They never think about alcohol unless they are actually busy drinking it.

Their morning-after-the-night-before, is not filled with self-recrimination or loathing.

They just pop a few aspirin and get on with their day.

Their life consists of plenty of other things,

They may shove a whole load of drink down their gullet, but I guarantee there's never been any navel-gazing, or dark night of the soul, regarding such actions.

They'll say things like *"I never had a hangover that wasn't worth it"* and they probably believe it, too.

In general, they are happy with their lot, and harbour no secret desire to change.

Could their quality of life be improved by less, or no alcohol consumption?

Probably.

Will they give it a moment's thought? Nah.

Because, like I say, they do not think about drinking unless they're actually doing it.

It just is what it is, and they're fine with that. Because, in the greater scheme of life? **They have never elevated alcohol to a place it does not belong.**

Therefore, alcohol plays are very small part in their *thoughts*, even if the *action* of drinking, potentially has massive ramifications on their mind, body, and interpersonal relationships.

In other words, somebody who is an authentic heavy drinker, will never read a book like this.

Why is it an inconvenient truth? *Because we like life to be black and white.*

Isn't it so much easier to believe that all alcohol abusers are bad. And that of course, alcohol is all-powerful and evil.

Because, if so, all we would have to do to achieve the perfect life, is use almighty willpower and stop drinking. No further personal development of self required!

Extreme views are rarely true. People with extreme views are rarely happy or peaceful.

*And the perfect life does not exist. Sober or drunk.*

Even though these authentic heavy drinkers may cause problems in the lives of those around them. They are at peace with their own behaviour. They're fine with it. And there will be no changing them.

They will die heavy drinkers, and never feel anything but satisfaction with their own lot.

*And not a single one of us has the right to sit in judgement over them, about that.*

I don't know about you, but I'm really pleased that I'm not one of them. I'm over-the-moon that I wasn't authentically at peace with my heavy-drinking situation, and that I was given the opportunity to discover who I really was.

Who I really am.

Now let's find out who you really are.

# CHAPTER 6

# Personal Preference Power

A couple of years went by, and I started to make more progress in my physical recovery.

But this progress was hard to maintain. My physical relapses would always follow the same sorry cycle.

I would bounce from bed, to wheelchair, to standing up, and even managing to take a few shuffling steps.

Aaaaaand then back to bed again.

Square one.

With the use of my arms and hands if I was lucky.

Yet this is a time in my life I am so thankful for. Because I experienced the most powerful lesson-and epiphany- that I've ever known, to this day.

This is where the crux of my **Shut Up, Alcohol!** method was born.

I discovered the awesome and unequivocal power of **forward moving**

**momentum.**

It is, without doubt, the single most important thing that I can teach you, so let's go!

Learning how to walk again is draining, to say the least.

It involves a lot of falling over, and then getting straight back up again, for more of the same.

Mentally it is draining. Physically it is painful.

But it's not the hardest part.

The hardest part about learning to walk is **standing still.**

This discovery blew my mind.

Re-learning to stand, is so very hard, that even to this day, all these years later, fully physically recovered, I have been known to occasionally struggle with it.

Whereas walking? Well, walking gets easier and easier and easier with every step.

And it's all thanks to the sheer power of **momentum**. That propelling forward, helps us in ways we never realise, until it is taken away.

*Cumulative forward motion is everything.*

And getting to physically embody this lesson? Changed. My. Life.

**Momentum** is the key. It's the code that, once cracked, opens every door imaginable.

(Harnessing the power of deliberate momentum, builds an incredible life. It goes way beyond simply the cessation of problem drinking. But that's something to consider at a later date. Let's get this part of the journey started for you, first.)

Yes, this was my seismic self-discovery.

*It was the biggest reason I had failed so miserably to stop drinking, using will power.*

And, conversely, why I was now achieving such great -yet, let's face it, somewhat baffling- success, with non-drinking. Despite the less-than-ideal personal circumstances I found myself in.

This is not just my personal truth; it applies to all of us.

To every single person, who has tried their damnedest to suddenly stop abusing alcohol, and "white knuckle" through each long day as a non-drinker, without any foresight or gameplan.

Learning how to walk, and struggling so badly with standing, had shown me why willpower *could never, and would never* work for me, as a long-term and legitimate method, to stop drinking.

# CHAPTER 7:

# Drinking Momentum?

# Or Non-Drinking Momentum?

We all have drinking thoughts. All of us who have a pattern of drinking to excess and feel unhappy about it. Every single one of us. It's not exactly breaking news that I'm sharing here, I know, but bear with me.

My biggest mistake, however, lay in assuming that my drinking thoughts *were only about when was I going to drink again, or how much should I drink at that moment.*

**When in reality, everything I was thinking, was actually a drinking thought**.

My hangovers contained drinking thoughts; My panic attacks contained drinking thoughts.

Every afternoon I spent mentally wrestling with myself, about what I was going to do that night?

I was actually having drinking thoughts.

To quote the great philosopher Estelle, *'I grew up in the 1980's.'*

When there were four terrestrial television channels. And they only played kids shows for a few hours every Saturday and Sunday morning.

As you can imagine, early Saturday mornings were a time of high excitement. A bowl of rice krispies in one hand. My Rainbow Brite doll in the other. I was all set: Let the good times roll.

I remember watching one, and it was about a cartoon dog trying to learn how to ski. He was very clumsy, (I can totally relate.) so his skis would get caught up under him. And down that ski slope he would tumble, a circular canine in motion.

He started off the downhill journey as a small snowball, but the further he rolled, the bigger and faster he got. Until eventually, this part hound, part icy aggregate mega sphere, swallowed up everything in its path. Consuming other skiers, animals, sledges, you name it.

That snowball was so now large and powerful, there was no stopping it, Incessant forward momentum pulling it down, at breakneck speed.

Until the inevitable tree collision, sending masses of broken, snowy destruction, everywhere.

Now, if you can, please cast your mind back to when you first started drinking. The inception of your drinking snowball if you will.

That first drink, and every subsequent one after it, started your own bespoke tiny snowball, rolling down life's hill.

Try to imagine every drink that followed. But not just the drinks. The hangovers. All of them. Every drinking-based drama that you were party to. Every night out that ended badly.

Every drunken trauma, experienced. Every fight, verbal or otherwise. These incidents that quickly become commonplace, only serve to make that snowball bigger.

The bigger and more uncontrollable it gets, the faster it rolls on, down the hill. Until, eventually, the speed gets too much.

We want out. And we try to counteract this gargantuan **Drinking Momentum** snowball, by building a new snowball, one we'll call **Non-Drinking Momentum**.

Imagine shouting instructions at the teeny, tiny new snowball.

Demanding that it immediately become as big, fast, and powerful as the one we spent so many years making?

We can't. It's just not happening.

It's not an overnight success job. But fortunately, there is a shortcut.

Because, yeah, we may have spent years making this truly terrifying Frankensnowball, that is now making life so difficult for us.

But we did it by default. And *any action done by default, instead of deliberately? Is never as powerful or effective.*

What an absolute bonus that is!

Now, all that is required, to play snowball catch-up, is strong, positive, deliberate, and consistent momentum.

Oh, and we need to stop giving any power whatsoever, to the old, **Drinking Momentum,** snowball.

Now, be honest, have I totally ruined winter for you yet?

No? Then let's continue.

See, it turns out, that in 2006, from the very first day of my non-drinking life, my "**I don't know**" conversations with my brain, were, in actual fact, the beginnings my little **Non-Drinking Momentum** snowball.

Every time I reaffirmed to myself that I didn't know why I couldn't drink anymore, I just absolutely knew that I couldn't. Not ever again. That was me, trying with all my might to get that lil' ball rolling.

(Totally by default, rather than design. Which is why it all took so bloody long to come together, but never mind. Hindsight is always

20/20. The main thing is, that you can now benefit from all that stumbling around that I did, and get to where I am, now, way faster than me, and with far more ease!)

I used most of my thoughts, from that point on in 2006, to help that nondrinking snowball, grow bigger and bigger.

Apart from the occasions that **Drinking Momentum** unwittingly snuck in without me noticing. Took me ages to identify the difference. But I did and I'll share how you can weed them out in the next chapter. Hint; it's such an important tool, it's also the book title… Anyway, back to the ball talk.

Now that I had finally identified the key to my present success (and realised the reason for my other past failures) in changing my heavy drinking ways?

That old **Drinking Momentum** could feck right off. I was done. It's days of wrecking, ruling, and controlling my life, were over, baby. Over!

I realised that throughout the years, though this giant snowball of Drinking Momentum had been massive, and too much for me to overcome without a proper framework?

Sooner or later it always broke apart on its own. The architect of its own destruction.

Those times when I would get too badly injured on a night out, to ignore. Miss too many days of work to go unnoticed. Behave in a way too unacceptable to brush under the carpet.

The abject horror of those incidents would stop any forward motion in its tracks. I would become frozen in fear. (Which explains why trying to scare ourselves sober is effective for a very short period of time.)

Then the ball would break apart and need *me* to come and put it back together, (which I always did, as soon as the effects of scaring myself sober would fade in my memory), so it could once again begin its destructive descent downhill.

Every single person reading this, has very strong **Drinking Momentum**, that is currently running every single *aspect* of their life. That snowball does not need them to keep it rolling, by now.

But sooner or later it will always hit something and break apart.

And the next time it does? We won't be putting it back together.

This time, it will stay broken, and disintegrate back into the ground, never to resurface again.

We will be calling the shots from now on. Instead of necking them, obviously.

From this moment on, we will give ourselves permission to be the one in charge.

## CHAPTER 8

## Shut Up, Alcohol!

Understanding whether we are contributing to our **Drinking Momentum**, or our **Non-Drinking Momentum**, is of paramount importance to easy, long-term success.

Which one are we actually giving our attention to? Which is getting larger and more powerful, right now? Taking in everything in its path?

*Because the truth is, we are always adding to one of them, every second of the day. With every thought and action. Deliberately, or by default.*

The good news is, now we know this for a fact, we can start and deliberately control our choices.

The *great news* is, we can start to disrupt the old thought cycles, immediately, without yet being an expert at identifying a **Drinking Momentum** thought, from a **Non-Drinking Momentum** thought.

Because, let me tell you, some of these thoughts are sneaky blighters. Masquerading as helpful, when, in reality, all they want is to keep us downtrodden and dependent on alcohol.

There are some Drinking Momentum thoughts which are really obvious.

*Brain:* **F*ck it, let's go have a drink** (Yeah, like we've ever had just one drink in the history of pressing the f*ck it button…)

*Brain:* **Might go out tonight for a bit** (it's a foregone conclusion by then, the only dishonest part is pretending the night will end early.)

*Brain:* **It's \_\_\_\_** *insert random, total non-occasion here **Everyone will be out, it's totally normal.** (just because something is common, doesn't make it normal, but okay.)

*Brain:* **I've had a bad day, I deserve this.** (Because drinking heavily is guaranteed to improve matters, right??)

*Brain:* **Looking forward to payday tomorrow!** (So that I can instantly squander all my wages on the only thing that makes me feel momentarily better about the crap life choices I continually make.)

*Brain:* **People will think I'm boring if I don't turn up.** (Really? Are we some A-List celebrity that people will door-watch for the entrance of, all night? Or will they barely register our non-appearance, in the grand scheme of things?

Also, we have very little trouble letting people down over plans that they try to make with us when they don't involve alcohol. Especially when we are hungover…just saying…)

The blatant Drinking thoughts that serve to top-up our **Drinking Momentum** are generally quite obvious.

You won't have any issue stopping those unhelpful thoughts in their tracks.

And how are you going to do that?

Catch that thought as it forms in your mind. The instant you become aware you are thinking it.

And, in your head, shout it with me: **SHUT UP, ALCOHOL!**

That's all we need do at this stage.

If you are at home, or want the person with no concept of personal space that is sat next to you on public transport, to go away? Say it out loud!

That's all it takes to shake things up in our brains. One sentence, said consistently, is all our inner self needs, to realise there is a new sheriff in town. One who takes no shit off anybody.

It's so simple and yet so effective, for two reasons:

1. **Drinking Momentum** weakens every time it is interrupted. Even before we get to the part where we deliberately switch our focus to **Non-Drinking Momentum**, instead. This disruption of the status quo sends our subconscious minds reeling. Which is exactly what we need.

2. We have spent years as repressed people-pleasers. Saying shut up to anyone is liberating. Saying it to the thing that has ruined us up until this point, is immensely satisfying. And it's about time we started letting

some pent-up emotions out, because we sure as hell won't be drinking them away any more...

Look, I get it. This is all a bit weird at first. And let's be clear. Alcohol has done many things to me in my lifetime, but it has yet to actually converse with me, not even in my wildest withdrawal hallucinations.

But anthropomorphising alcohol is an important part of this method. It's vital in helping to weed out **Drinking Momentum**, from **Non-Drinking Momentum**. Which is genuinely a skill that few of us master, without solid framework.

Now, onto the trickier part of this new tool: identifying **Drinking Momentum** that disguises itself as **Non-Drinking Momentum**...

The upsetting thing about this subgroup of thoughts, is that we use them with all the best intentions. Then blame ourselves when willpower and discipline don't keep us away from the temptation of booze.

It breaks my heart to think of the amount of people who have lost time, opportunities, relationships, their health, wellbeing, even their lives. All because they didn't know that certain thoughts only make our drinking behaviours worse.

I'm going to list some of the common and worst offenders of this category. Some of them might surprise you.

*Brain:* **I'm not drinking tonight.**

This insidious phrase is harmful on so many levels. Let's examine a couple of them in detail:

- Our Brain filters for the words *drink* and *tonight* first and foremost. Our synapses fire off all sorts of sepia-toned drinking montages. The **Drinking Momentum** couldn't be moving faster now if we stuck it to the front of a juggernaut.

- When chronic uncertainty and powerlessness are ingrained responses, we stick silent questions marks at the end of every sentence. There are no statements. Only questions and begging of permission that is never granted. ***I'm not drinking tonight?*** Oh yes you are…

*Brain:* **I've been sober for ___ amount of days**

You know who counts days? *Prisoners.* Short term its fine, I did it myself for three months because I thought I had to. Long term it only ensures we are never free of alcohol's clutches.

Imagine if I was to wake up every day and remind myself how long it had been since my last drink. Bloody hell, how grim.

Me: *Looks in mirror: **Day number 6221, Congratulations, Carrie's face.***

(Just worked it out, took me flipping ages too, maths is deffo not my strong point).

Why would we count anything unless we are expecting it to end? I will be a non-drinker for eternity. Why do I need a running total?

*Brain: **If I get through this weekend without drinking, I'm going to treat myself.***

Treat yourself anyway. And aim way higher. Because let's just say we were even into using unhelpful phrases like this one, its *"when'*, not *'if"* …

Conditional self-love leads to judgement, berating and then right back to drinking. Whereas unconditional self-love is a powerful tool indeed.

*Brain: **I'm so hungover/I can't believe what I did last night/ oh my god I can't remember anything at all. I'm never drinking again. I mean it this time!***

Shaming, as a tool, lasts about as long as the panic or hangover does. So good luck with that. We've all tried it. None of us succeeded.

As soon as the idea of alcohol/lack of alcohol, worms its way into our mind, the path is pre-determined. We cannot stop drinking if we let any notion of booze even take root. The only way to start vital **Non-Drinking Momentum**, at first, is to create a completely alcohol-free mind.

(Later on in the journey, this is no longer relevant. But we must work through this stage, to progress to the next.)

So, to recap: Anything to do with drinking, can only ever add to the strong **Drinking Momentum** we have spent years building up.

Alcohol. Hangovers. Obsessing over days. Literally anything remotely to do with drinking or trying to "give up" is a futile endeavour.

Tell every single one of those thoughts **SHUT UP, ALCOHOL!** Because as long as we continue to think them? Even a little bit? Alcohol is still the CEO of our mind.

There are people who have been non-drinkers for years that still spend every single minute of every single day, unwittingly building up **Drinking Momentum**. No wonder they feel so vulnerable to relapse.

By the way, I have nothing but pure admiration for anyone who has managed to stop drinking and keep doing it, in this way. What a bloody hard slog that must be. No wonder I couldn't hack it.

I'll stick to the effortless way though, ta.

I can only imagine how exhausting it must feel, to be pulling in the opposite direction, of the very thoughts that are supposed to be helping me.

The worst that can happen is the downhill pull becomes so strong, they succumb to it.

The best scenario is they are strong enough to pull against, but not create any momentum in the opposite, Non-Drinking direction.

Which must mean they are **Standing Still**.

And, as I learned in my own life. Standing still is the hardest skill to master, of all.

Hopefully, at this stage, it is becoming clear to you, why stopping drinking has been such an almighty struggle, in the past.

Though I understand that it's also confusing.

**Because what is there, apart from Drinking Momentum, if all alcohol/sobriety- centric thoughts are only adding to the problem?**

Let me be blunt here: You currently think very few thoughts that aren't in these two categories. Otherwise, you wouldn't have found this book in the first place.

*When we elevate alcohol to a place it does not belong? Life becomes warped.*

Our circle of experience gets smaller and smaller, as our drinking problem gets bigger and bigger.

In fact, the easiest way to spot if someone has an alcohol problem, or not, is to get them to list things that have nothing to do with alcohol, or sober living.

In reality **Non-Drinking Momentum** completely dwarfs **Drinking Momentum**. It is absolutely everywhere we turn, in every single part of the world.

But we have trained ourselves to see the exact opposite.

Us folk who fixate on alcohol and sobriety, (both drinking obsessed thoughts), believe the ultimate truth is that the entire world revolves around drinking and getting drunk.

Which is a massive lie.

I used to buy into that falsehood, too.

Luckily it doesn't take long to disprove.

I'm so totally indifferent to alcohol now, that I don't see it anywhere. Even when it is right in front of me, I subconsciously filter it out. On television, in restaurants, at parties. You name it, I'm oblivious to it.

To the point where, I actually did a guest spot on a sober-living webinar, whilst

sat in front of a cabinet, filled to the brim with every bottle of spirits imaginable. *In a flatshare I had lived in for two years.*

It was in my own living room, yet I had walked past it several times a day, and not even registered it.

The evidence of my indifference to alcohol? Indisputable!

The live comments? Awkward!

I could argue that my personal truth, is that alcohol no longer exists. Because it may as well not, as far as my eyes and mind are aware.

In fact, I often say, that as far as I am concerned, everyone in the world stopped drinking on the day I did. Because their drinking is now genuinely invisible to me.

But I'm jumping way ahead now.

Let's get back to the 99.9% of our planetary content, that has nothing to do with obsessing over alcohol, or a lack thereof.

People, places, and things that we have spent so many years ignoring, we have become unable to even see them.

It's time to play **The Opposite Game**.

# CHAPTER 9

# The Opposite Game

Let's go back to our chat about being authentic Non-Drinkers.

As I mentioned earlier, we authentic Non-Drinkers actually feel a sense of peace, possibly for the first time in our lives, because we are finally living our truth.

The reason we have been feeling so bad and disliking ourselves so very much over these long years.

Is because we have been living lives that weren't truly ours.

This alcohol habit, or addiction, (whatever you choose to call it) that's been taking centre stage for so long? It's not a true reflection of our genuine inner selves.

It's nothing to do with our actual values, or beliefs. This habit has nothing to do with us, at our core. That is why we have felt no peace for years, if ever. There is no personal power in living a way that isn't true to us.

I bring up **The Opposite Game** now, because it feeds in so well, to creating powerful, new **Non-Drinking Momentum**.

Now, all this talk of inner true inner selves and authentic living, is well and good. But they're just lofty concepts, really, (powerful, mind you. One's that have played a significant part in changing my life. Still, just ethereal ideas, all the same. And I'm not here to talk about airy fairy, vague, wishy-washy notions.)

You came here for tools. So, practical tools are what you are going to get. As heavy drinkers, we feel bad pretty much all of the time.

Not just the time devoted to drinking. Nor simply those hours that we are hungover or panicking. Wracked with guilt and shame.

All. Of. The. Time.

It's the devil you know. We get so used to feeling awful, it becomes like a security blanket. We are comforted by its dreadful familiarity.

We become so adept at feeling rubbish; we forget there is any other way. But all that is about to change.

Newsflash: **Most humans roam the earth, free from feeling terrible about themselves, and their actions. And without feeling constant physical distress from hangovers, or mentally enervated by beer fear**.

I know, right? I was surprised by this information too, at first.

Having an intolerance to feeling bad, is an excellent gift that we can give ourselves, and we can start and cultivate a sense of that *right now*.

These days, I too have an absolute intolerance to feeling bad, and fixating on negativity.

It turns out, that underneath all the drinking related dross, the real, authentic me is naturally drawn towards feeling good.

I really like thinking upbeat thoughts and having a positive outlook. It's hard work to get myself in any other frame of mind. And even if I can persuade myself to, I cannot stay there long.

Drinking me, non-authentic me, was the most cynical person on the face of the Earth.

It was something that people told me often.

Believe it or not, I took that as a compliment. Goodness knows why.

My alcohol consumption made me negative. It depressed me, literally. My brain chemistry was a total mess.

And since we can only interpret anything, through our own emotional guidance system, my worldview, beliefs, and perspectives increasingly became negatively warped.

**My personality became nothing more than a physiological response to my alcohol consumption**.

It wasn't me. Never had been. And, thankfully, it never would be again. How could I possibly have felt any different, under such restrictive circumstances?

I gave myself absolutely no option, or opportunity, to discover that my authentic self was in fact the polar opposite to how I was currently living and feeling.

*Any time we feel bad, we are behaving as, or believing in, something that is in direct opposition to who we really, truly are*.

No ifs. No but's. No exceptions.

To this day, a strong negative inner response, tells me I am acting or thinking in a way that is untrue to my core self. And this is 17 years down the line from alcohol abuse, so, as the Andrex adverts of the glorious 1980's said, you know this tool is for life, not just for Christmas…

And so it goes, that any time I'm feeling bad, limited, or just "off", I know it's time to play The Opposite Game. Because my brain is using negative feelings, to try and communicate with me, so I can, in return, give it the support it needs.

Back in my early days of non-drinking, my mind was very

uncomfortable with such an abrupt change of routine.

It tried every trick in the book to sound the alarm. Attempted to get me so anxious, that I would do whatever it took, to revert my world back to the small, and therefore manageable, place it interpreted as safe.

And *nothing makes a world smaller than alcohol abuse*. So, no wonder my mind wanted me drunk again, as soon as possible!

Thankfully, my mind learned that I no longer need protecting from my own behaviour anymore, and pretty soon yours will know that you don't, either. Result!

**Non-Drinking Momentum** is about what feels authentically good, for us.

What will make us feel genuinely enthused and inspired.

Happy, fulfilled, loved, and immersed in life's wonderful, never-ending variety of experiences.

**And the fool-proof way to do this at first, is by choosing the polar opposite of what we think we need, to keep us safe, right now.**

For example, let's say your brain is used to going to the pub on a Friday night (we'll keep this example as functional as possible, and leave alone the more niche dysfunctional experiences, that our brains have long justified as normal. Pretty much all of us have had our minds try and take us out on the piss, of a weekend night, right?)

Your Brain: *Woohoo, it's Friday night beeyach! We got through another shite week; we deserve to let our hair down*!

You: *Oh, well I don't think we should-*

Your Brain: *Don't be ridiculous! Everyone's going. We'll miss out. God you're so boring, no wonder everyone hates us. Etc.*

Our brain is taking proper liberties here, and no mistake. It has clearly teamed up with the giant bottle of alcohol that I like to chat with, regularly. Let's put them both in a place with a…

You: **SHUT UP, ALCOHOL!**

Yeah, that's sorted them right out. Cheeky blighters.

So, we've disrupted that unhelpful thinking pattern. Stopped it right in its tracks. Go us!

It's now time to play **The Opposite Game** and set the tone for some brilliant, new, deliberate, **Non-Drinking Momentum.**

For a start, the authentic version of you is not missing out on a damn thing by sitting in the same lame pub, or club, having the same tired conversations, repeatedly.

If anything, authentic you is missing out by wasting it's Friday night getting drunk, not to mention the rest of the written-off-by-another-hangover-weekend.

Missing out on being with the right people. Doing things that you truly would enjoy and feel fulfilled by. Even if you don't know fully what those things are, just yet.

Missing out because you're showing up to someone else's life. A life that you never consciously set out to choose.

A life that does not feel good to you.

And a life that is hurting you, on every level.

So what does the authentic you want?

What is authentic non-drinking behaviour for you? Well, keeping it simple as its early days:

*The opposite of the Friday night location, that so often ends badly, is going to a place that is not alcohol centric. Or staying in, providing the environment is beautiful and relaxing.*

So where do people go, and what do people do when they either don't drink or are indifferent to alcohol?

You'll know, or know of, at least one person who is a non-drinker.

They will go to the cinema, play sports, go to the gym. Stay in and pamper themselves. Buy in their favourite snacks, and binge on a new Netflix series.

Deliberate non-drinkers, do things that feed their soul, during their relaxation time. **Things that *feel* good to them, not that *look* good to others.**

Successful non-drinkers, always have at least one hobby on the go, even if they are just trying it out for size.

Honestly? I still flounder without a framework. I like to have at least one firm plan each day. Maybe I'm still trying to make constructive use of my time, to make up for all the years I wasted, staring down the bottom of so many pint glasses.

(Let me point out here, that I don't need this rigid framework because I will drink without it, though. I need it because I stopped drinking late in life and missed out on all-self-starter skills, because **No Manual**. I want to get the most out of my life, not simply achieve the status of long-term non-drinking.)

Anyway, back to hobbies, and such. They can just be small behaviour changes at first, we're not talking about a complete lifestyle overhaul. It's coming, but not yet.

Now, what would **The Opposite Game** involve, instead of a Saturday and Sunday morning, spent hiding under the duvet with a killer hangover?

**The opposite of a drinker is a do-er**.

Non-drinkers get up. Show up. Go out. They are curious about the world that surrounds them, so they explore it, little by little.

The opposite of a restrictive hungover, or alcohol fuelled weekend?

Is a free, wide-reaching agenda, full of variety.

And if you want to start and connect with the authentic you. The one who has been waiting in the wings, eager to get involved?

Just cast your mind back to things that you did as a teenager, before you discovered alcohol.

Now, before you go get your best Take That posters out of storage or start applying your finest Collection 2000 Heather shimmer lipstick, set off nicely with a few liberal sprays of Sun-In, to your freshly permed barnet?

We don't have to be quite so literal about this. Finding the feeling place of how our leisure time used to be, is enough.

I used to go to dance classes with my mates. After which, we would hang around in city centre cafes for hours, trying to stretch out one soft drink between us all.

But the *feeling place* that was most useful for me to recreate. The opposite of how drinking always made me feel. Was a sense of never clock watching. Never caring what time, it was. Just letting time do whatever it wanted, without trying to control any of it, or make it bend to my anxious needs. The total relief of a quiet mind.

I'll never forget a lady I did Skype sessions with, years ago.

She was brilliant. Razor-sharp wit. Intelligent, searingly honest. A great businesswoman. Very kind. Really, so much going for her.

But she was convinced she had to hang on to her problem drinking. Because she would never find love again, without it. Because her current truth was, that men only find drinkers attractive.

A very untrue, not to mention, unhelpful belief, but there you go...

She was 100% convinced, that drinking was what made her attractive. Despite it being one of the reasons her husband cited, when he filed for divorce.

In between our sessions, this lady had made stunning progress in the areas where most of us flounder, at first.

She had embraced trying new hobbies, with incredible aplomb.

And her amazing ability to organise non-alcohol centric events, with friends and family in full attendance, was borderline military. All done without a hint of apology or self-consciousness.

Things would be going beautifully. Until she would freak out and end up going to get drunk with the first loser gent who give her a wink, on the dating app she frequented.

Did she like any of them? No.

Did she even fancy them, even a bit? Also no.

Well, okay, but did she at least get any enjoyment out of going back to drinking, after learning to live very well without it?

No! She hated the drinking part the most. Didn't miss it at all. Couldn't begin to imagine why she had wasted so many decades, and a half-decent marriage by choosing booze instead.

But so desperate was she, to be accepted by any man at all, that it was what she currently valued, far more than her own happiness and self-worth.

And there was no convincing her otherwise. This was going to have to be a self-taught lesson. A personal epiphany. Nothing else would undo such powerful self-talk.

On the off-chance, I asked her to go back to a time and she was a non-drinker. This is something many of us cannot remember in any great detail.

But what was unusual about this lady, was she started drinking later in life, in her mid-twenties. Not like so many of us, who start our journey with alcohol as young teenagers.

She was reluctant to talk or think about the past, as so much of it was tied up in memories of her ex-husband, which was totally understandable.

But this day, she decided to describe the outfits she and her friends used to wear

(Ps: top tip: beautiful outfits are always a winning choice in **The Opposite Game**). How they would put on these designer garments and have amazing adventures on the Kings Road in West London. Or the huge dinner parties they would attend.

How she would love chatting to everyone and flit from table to table, so she could enjoy meeting the most people.

**And how easy and fun it was to be able to fit in a good, proper conversation with everyone she wanted, because she used to love drinking fizzy pop out of glass bottles, whilst everyone else got drunk instead.**

And there it was. A memory buried by decades of alcohol abuse. She loved the freedom of non-drinking. Her friends would poke fun at her for being like a kid, but she knew they were all jealous of her ability to socialise so well.

She was, as it turns out, drinking lemonade the night she met her ex-husband.

Witnessing the moment that she remembered the authentic version of herself. That truly awesome realisation and reconnection, after so long?

The memory of it still gives me goosebumps.

Words can never teach as powerfully as real-life experiences. (This is such an inconvenient truth to point of half-way through a book, why am I like this, please? Let's get back to the story...)

In that moment she instantly dropped the loser men, as well as the untrue belief that all men want, is a woman who drinks heavily.

And once again became the happy, pop supping, social butterfly, she had been as a young woman.

Reconnecting with her authentic, non-drinking self, was all the assurance she needed, that this was the right path for her.

It is my firm belief that, just like pop lady, we all have a similar version of ourselves. One that possibly has never even had the chance to do anything except lie dormant, so far.

But they are still always trying to contact to us in some way. That the real us, lies just beneath all the horrible self-talk, the trauma, and other crap. Beneath the drama and the bad habits, we picked up, to try and numb ourselves to it all.

Ready to take the wheel, just as soon as we decide it is safe to let them.

And now feels like as good a time as any.

# CHAPTER 10

# Let's get shouty.

As mentioned earlier, I didn't call this method **Shut Up, Alcohol!** due to any delusions that bottles of booze hold regular conversations with any of us.

But there's something deeply satisfying, about being able to finally *shut up* those damn incessant drinking thoughts, after so many years at their mercy.

I know from personal experience, that starting to shout *shut up* at my own brain, before projecting that anger onto something that felt more "outside of me", only served to crush my already low self-esteem.

All alcohol abusers have low self-esteem. Happy people don't harm themselves.

Put themselves in risky situations. Compromise their interpersonal relationships. They just don't. So yeah, we all have chronically bad self-esteem in the early days of non-drinking.

And if I ask you to shout *shut up* to your own brain whilst you still feel this way? No long-lasting alliance between the two parts of us, (authentic self, and heavy drinking self.) can ever be forged.

We are the vehicle that alcohol needs. The show doesn't run without us. It took losing the use of my hands for some time, to appreciate I was the only one who used to physically pour alcohol down my own throat. It was me, every single time, whether it felt like it, or not,

All that time I spent unable to move my body, or care for myself, alcohol never broke into my bedroom and demanded we party together.

No, it stayed in its bottle, and left me the hell alone.

Part of taking control of our lives and our destiny, is to be the one in charge. To be the grown-up in the room.

Many of us have never felt like the grown-up in the room because: **No Manual**. Living a fully rounded life as an authentic non-drinker, gives us the great opportunity for autonomy.

After years of not being the boss, because we didn't want to come across as bossy.

As people pleasers, this can feel uncomfortable. Especially since we instinctively want to stop everyone being mad at us, when we get drunk and misbehave, with such regularity. Malleability becomes a response and a coping mechanism.

But it's worth it, all in the name of personal growth. So, let's go!

As you saw in earlier chapters, I started off by shouting *shut up* to my brain, rather than to alcohol. I mean, it works, but it slowed down my progress massively, and hammered my already low sense of self-worth, so I wouldn't recommend it in the early days.

When the drinking thoughts come, learning to say **Shut Up, Alcohol!** helps sift through and identify which thoughts are true to us, and what is just our fear of change. Or, in other words, that which is innately within us, our beautiful, whole selves, versus our problematic behaviour. Which is definitely separate to us and can always be changed under the right circumstances

Imagining it is literally the bottle of alcohol itself, that is trying to persuade us back to a life of self-harm and destruction, whilst admittedly is a bit of a random way to go about things, is very effective for identifying and separating ourselves, from our actions.

Who we are versus what we do.

Most importantly, it has worked, for a lot of women, over a lot of years. Me being one of them.

By saying **Shut Up, Alcohol!** we physically choose new things to pour down our throat. So that's good.

But that is a tiny, insignificant part of the process. What we are really doing, is choosing to embrace time.

As heavy drinkers, we are afraid of having any spare time on our hands, so we fill it with drinking, or distract ourselves with hangovers.

For anyone living a life of dysfunction, free time is the enemy. It leads to all sorts of introspection. Very uncomfortable stuff altogether. Far better we open another bottle and get rid of those nasty truths, eh?

I too, was so scared of spare time.

And then I found myself in a position where I was in a bed, and I physically couldn't move. In these circumstances, distraction was no longer an option.

So I decided to embrace time, make it my friend, using **The Opposite Game**, to *feel* good, even when I couldn't *think* constructively.

I could not stop time from marching on, robbing me of the years I should have been embracing life, fully, as a non-drinker. But I could practise in my mind, for the day I was able to leave the house and finally do more than exist.

And that day finally came.

Finally, I was able to consistently walk, leave the house, and care for myself enough, that I did not need carers anymore.

I was able to control my body and go out into the world.

But what did I want to do with my life? How did I want to show up? How did I want to participate in this big wide world. Now that I was no longer a drinker, but a do-er?

I decided to become a TV presenter.

I moved hundreds of miles, down to London, (against medical advice, which was to stay living in my parent's spare room, do some volunteering a few afternoons a week, and wait for the next cycle of physical relapse to begin.)

There is absolutely nothing wrong with a life like that.

I just knew that it wasn't for me and that my deliberate **Non-Drinking Momentum** needed more than this, to keep building.

And to do so effectively, I needed to form some strong personal preferences. Stronger than, be able to walk and leave the house, which is all I had so far. Due to being exposed to so little of the world, for years.

London was a big place. Big enough for me to never have to go near any of my old drinking haunts from my drama school days, thank goodness.

And I found myself able to try new things all of the time, whether it was a one-off event, or a more regular activity.

I was no longer an actor, and never felt the desire to go back to it once I stopped drinking. Maybe I now had an intolerance to pretending at all anymore, who knows?

But I still loved the theatre, So I started reviewing plays and musicals for a theatrical website, on my free afternoons or evenings off work.

I was really interested in personal development, so would join local groups of like-minded people, and swap ideas with them.

I enjoyed going out for afternoon tea with the new friends I was making, on my day jaunts around London.

My new best friend, who would soon become my flatmate, I met when we sat next to each other in a nail bar.

A very different sort of bar than I would have historically made friends in…

Physically I was still trying to build my strength back up, whilst trying to find out who the real me was, and what she liked. So, I decided to kill two birds with one stone, and went on a yoga holiday.

Where I made the very valuable discovery, that I am terrible at yoga.

And I really do not enjoy it.

Had I attended one single class before booking a week-long yoga holiday in Turkey? Why no. No, I did not.

Should I have possibly done so? Why yes. Yes, I should.

In fact, so awful was I at yoga, that the Turkish yoga teachers re-named me *"Carrie, no yoga"* for the duration of my stay.

Despite the hours I spent hating my life doing yoga, badly, every day. I had a truly brilliant time.

I made great new friends. Ate new food I would never have otherwise tried. Saw a beautiful part of the world I had never been to before and gained great self-esteem by going so far out of my comfort zone.

My new, strong, and very clear personal preference was for *no yoga, ever again*. And that's fine, that's more than okay, **because I loved every aspect of the journey, that got me to that place of discovering what I didn't like.**

As far as **Non-Drinking Momentum** goes, I will never be able to give you a better, or more fully rounded example, than that.

# CHAPTER 11

# Filtering

I stopped drinking right before the invention of Facebook.

Which meant I was navigating the early days as a non-drinker, whilst simultaneously getting to grips with rudimentary social media.

I've talked about filtering for years as a means to further develop good momentum. But it's only as social media has evolved, that it has become such an easy tool to understand.

We all know the power of hashtags, and how they can quickly provide so many useful examples of what we are searching online for.

In some ways, social media can be a great and powerful tool to help with **Non-Drinking Momentum.**

As long as, (yes, you've guessed it), we don't specifically search for sober type "inspiration" Because, of course, we now know how much it unfortunately, only serves to speed up our old **Drinking Momentum.**

There's nothing wrong with people feeling pride in beating addiction. Every milestone can be celebrated, and why not?

I'm not saying any method that is not mine, is the wrong way to stop drinking. There are no wrong ways to do it, and anyone that tells you their way is the only way? Please run away in the opposite direction from them, as fast as you can!

There are tons of ways to stop drinking. More than I could ever count. And not just because I failed my GCSE Maths, three times.

All I'm saying is, why not bring a bit of ease into the situation.

Peer support groups are an amazing thing.

And, of course, Alcoholics Anonymous is one of the longest serving peer groups in existence.

I see nothing wrong with attending Alcoholics Anonymous meetings.

Especially in the early days, when we feel a strong need to identify with our new community and want to hear all about other people stories.

There are people who have used the **Shut Up, Alcohol!** method in the past and quite happily attended AA meetings too, at first. Not just AA, either. Local peer support groups and community incentives.

As long as a person is abstinent from alcohol consumption, I feel confident in saying they will be welcome in most recovery-based groups.

This is not true for people working on controlling alcohol though, so please don't expect them to change their rules for you.

Which is the main reason why, after a lot of soul-searching, I decided that a method for controlling alcohol, had to be included in this book.

Even though I well-know what the fall-out from it will be.

Too many women are lying about being fully sober and feel secretly ashamed about it.

Too many of us are living in isolation. Shunned by those in recovery, yet unable to be with the problem drinkers, they used to surround themselves with.

Too many people who could, (with a very rigid framework), successfully drink small amounts, will go back to abusing alcohol. Because this in-between place is a lonely sort of purgatory, with only the judgement of others to keep them company.

Just because I choose not to drink at all, doesn't mean I get to decide how another woman chooses to be indifferent to alcohol.

Think of the handful of tools I am giving you in this book, as some of the weapons in your warrior queen arsenal.

But they don't have to be the only weapons!

The great thing about a self-support structures like mine, is that you can very easily complement it with support groups, or with therapy sessions, heck, why not both!

Having experienced long periods of total isolation, and their horror, I would never recommend any tool or method that could only be used, solo.

Nothing great happens in isolation. And, much as I made some wonderful discoveries during my terrible years of being housebound. Each one took a long, long time. Because anything that happens in isolation, with no one to bounce ideas off, is slow-going.

It's as close to standing still as you can get, really.

That's why, although I did not originally invent this method as a way to control alcohol, whilst still drinking it. I very much respect the ladies that can, and do, choose to use it, in this way.

As long as they have done the work, and remain genuinely indifferent to alcohol, at all times.

It is easy for other people to overpower and influence us if we don't know who we are, or what we want. But if we are strong and certain in ourselves, and deliberately build strong, new personal preferences?

The white noise of things that are no longer relevant, automatically gets filtered out, and permanently so.

To the point where, you too may just find yourself accidentally doing a webinar, with a backdrop of spirit bottles you didn't even know were in your own house...

Filters are fine, just use them to look for new hobbies and enhance your creativity, not for supposed "sober inspiration", and you'll be grand.

But let's get offline and take an example from the real world. Because successful **Non-Drinking Momentum** is not made by hiding at home behind a phone screen!

Now, let's say we've played **The Opposite Game**, to establish what an enjoyable, life affirming way to spend the evening would be, and your brain has helpfully told us to go to a nice restaurant, with a friend.

Your brain gave you lovely, firm criteria, like what sort of food, ambience, outfit, mocktails, etc. even which friend!

It's me, I'm that friend. Hello friend, nice to meet you.

So, here we are, in this lovely restaurant, how nice! Look at us, feeling all pretty and smelling *great* obviously, because no more minging alcohol fug surrounds us.

Neither of us is hungover, yay! So, we are really excited to eat. The waiter has taken our food order, and we are both having a virgin Nojito (my personal favourite of all mocktails), there is a slight lull in conversation, so we both look around.

What do you see? What's the first thing your eye lands on?

This is important because it's the most accurate indicator of your current mindset.

There are literally thousands of things in this place full of people and objects. So, what gets your attention?

Let me tell you precisely what my eyeballs would have zoned in on, during one of my very few trips out, in the six weeks I tried using willpower alone to stop drinking:

I would have noticed what everyone else was drinking.

I would have noticed everyone that looked a lot better than me.

I would have noticed anyone seemingly having a better time than me.

I would have noticed where the exits were in case I had one of my frequent panic attacks.

I would have noticed any clock on a wall, as it would reveal to me how long there was to go until I could escape. Just in case tonight was the night I broke down, gave in, and started drinking again.

Back then, my absolute truth, that was reflected to me, everywhere I looked, was that alcohol was everywhere. And everyone was drinking and having a better time than me.

Total bull, obviously.

But let's fast forward to all of these years later. Back to you and I being friends and building lovely **Non-Drinking Momentum** together.

What am I looking at? What's automatically my biggest point of attraction? What am I filtering for?

Well, there's me, because I actually count these days. So, I'm appreciating the lovely clothes that I'm wearing, that I got myself because I show up to work and get paid. And I spend money on clothes because I no longer ruin them by destroying them on chaotic nights out.

Maybe I look down and see my nice nails that I now spend time and money on. Not like when I used to bite them right down as a drinker. Yet another chronic habit I broke instantly as a non-drinker.

Then my eyes drift to the surrounding tables, taking in the plates of food I see on them, because I love food so much these days. No longer is it the enemy it once was on so many levels.

I see people at tables, enjoying each other's company. It reminds me of my wonderful husband, and how blessed we are to have such a great marriage.

Now, I'm looking to the outskirts of the room, getting a full view of the decor, because I'm super into interiors these days. Unlike the vile surroundings I created in my drinking days. When I was not the only thing in my flat suffering from severe neglect.

**I'm looking for things that make me feel good. Instead of using everything I can see, as a stick to beat myself up with and feel bad about.**

That is the power of filtering.

There will be alcohol in this room. But it holds no interest for me. I genuinely won't register seeing it. Such is the command of indifference.

What do I mean by that? Think of something that will be in every restaurant you've ever been to and will ever go to.

But it's of absolutely no consequence to you, or your experience there.

The waitress's notepad. What style of water jug is on your table. If you are a meat eater, what their vegetarian menu consists of. These things exist in tandem with our own dining experience, but they are wholly irrelevant.

That's how I feel about alcohol in restaurants. That's what indifference feels like.

You experience indifference every single day, and have done your entire life, so it's entirely possible to cultivate a sense of this indifference, deliberately, towards alcohol.

It's the same as having no opinion. Something increasingly rare these days, five minutes on Twitter/X will prove that.

As a successful non-drinker I have three settings nowadays:

1. I really like something; it's a strong personal preference and I incorporate it into my life often to make it an even better place.
2. I am indifferent to it, and it doesn't exist for me.

3. I see an injustice, do what I can to be of service, then go straight back to living my best, happy life.

I don't get outraged for the sake of it. I never ruminate on negativity, just to make idle conversation.

And I don't get any sense of satisfaction from people thinking I am hard done by or brave for not drinking.

The stuff that other people get all het up about? Very rarely registers with me, not anymore. And that is the freedom that comes of indifference. We get to focus on the stuff that we really have authentically driven opinions about.

And leave the rest well enough alone.

As society has evolved; every day outrage has become something that makes money and provides leverage. We can choose to not be a part of that. To have an easy, effortless life experience, instead.

The early days of non-drinking do contain anger. I often think it is because we never got to be angry little emo-type teenagers, seeing as we were far too busy being drunk ones…

Because whilst other people were trying to save the whale or the rainforest, or their local youth centre. All we cared about was where our next bottle of 20/20 was coming from.

When we become non-drinkers, we have to start developing emotions at the age we Arrested Development at, that usually involves a bit of teenage rebellion.

Which is part of the reason I became a militant vegan in my late twenties. It was a rite of passage I had to go through too, and I did it for years. Turns out it wasn't the real me, just a natural phase. Albeit a decade after everyone else around me had experienced theirs…

These days my life is one big happy place, where all the things I love and everything I like are constantly reflected back to me as my centre of attention.

And I dislike so few things, that they don't tend to register with me. Turns out most of my negative thoughts were **Drinking Momentum** ones, so you can imagine how long it's been since I had any of that momentum going.

# CHAPTER 12

# The myth of perfection

We really need to talk about the myth of perfection. And how it will try to sabotage every attempt at being a non-drinker, you will ever make, unless you kick it to the curb.

My own impossible quest for perfection, became a serious pitfall that derailed me for years. Not in the sense that I started drinking again. But it made my life hell for a long time.

Whilst it was a great learning curve for me, I'd still much prefer you to learn from my story, rather than from repeating my actions.

Perfection does not exist. What I was actually chasing was a blank, sterile life where nothing ever changed.

My big quest originally was to stop drinking. Such an impossible dream for years, until it happened! Then I was happy.

For five whole minutes.

I stopped smoking the same day I stopped drinking, because it was the combination of both, that did it for me. One without the other was useless, that's what I told myself.

In retrospect I was chasing the high of perfection from day one.

Very soon afterwards, I got so unwell, I could not physically feed myself.

I could choose to eat some of what people tried to feed me or refuse to eat at all. Those were my choices. And I hated it.

Eventually I did get the use of my hands, back, if not my legs. So, the internet became my newest buddy.

I would fill my search engine with phrases like *"why can't I walk now?"* and *"How do I recover?"*

And of course, you put a combination of words like that into the internet, even back in 2007, there was only one type of response.

The wellness, diet and health industries, all reared up and smacked me in the face, for the first time in my life.

I thought to myself *my God look at how terribly I've been treating my body*, finding this comforting and familiar pattern of guilt and shame in blaming myself for my current circumstances. Despite them having no root in drinking, or hangovers at all.

There and then I dived straight into disordered eating, into what was referred to as clean eating, back in the day. But of course, like any good alcohol abuser, I took it to the absolute extreme.

I was utterly fixated on my diet, obsessed with what I consumed. All of my deliberate momentum went there, and I developed an eating disorder called Orthorexia Nervosa, a whole new eating disorder snowball.

Rolling that snowball took my attention away from creating a lovely new life, for years. Even after I was truly well and had my physical freedom back.

What I ate became my whole identity. All of my attention was on what went into my mouth. Instead of the things I said and did, that came out of it. That's a fairly messed-up set of values to have. Not to mention, exhausting.

So many women fall into the trap of clean or mythologically perfect eating, in the early days of non-drinking. It's a sure-fire way back to the bottle. Please don't do it.

Let's go through a mini life cycle of the penitent perfectionist:

Imagine, if you will, that it's a typical early Sunday evening.

You've been caning it like a rugby team on a stag do, Friday through to early hours of Sunday morning.

Your mate, good old beer fear himself, has decided to pay a visit, and the feelings of paranoia and panic are borderline unbearable.

That's it! You can't take anymore! This week will be different. You cower under your duvet and pray for the new day, with its chance of a brand-new start, to arrive soon.

*Monday morning.* Yay! So early do you rise! So virtuous do you feel, that you shun that usual cup of coffee! No longer will your body be a vessel for caffeinated muck!

Water is the only beverage to pass your lips. Food will be a salad, no dressing.

So fixated are you on your own goodness, the day flies by. Off to the supermarket to load up on plant-based food and fruit (but not high calorie stuff like bananas, obvs.) in bed by 8 o'clock, hungry, bored, but glowing with self-satisfaction.

*Tuesday morning* sees you hungry but not hungover, yaaaasss! Work is work, straight home to peruse social media, where absolutely everyone in the entire universe is having a good time except you.

Bed by 7 o'clock. Alone and irritated.

*Wednesday* is more starvation, and the prospect of yet more isolation.

Until someone suggests heading to the pub after work, where you get bladdered because you've eaten nothing for days, black out, and hopefully don't hurt yourself, just hate yourself, all over again.

Thankfully there's a tool to counteract the myth of perfection.

It doesn't have a name, but every single woman I have ever taught it to, has hated it, so I started referring to it as **that tool you hate**, and it stuck.

# CHAPTER 13

# That tool you hate

It's not fancy. It's not even difficult. Unless you've got a background of binge then-atone, like all of us problem drinkers do. In which case I am about to ask a hell of a lot of you, soz.

Firstly, I'm going to ask you to eat like a regular human.

Without restriction. Without rules. Without obsession. Lots of people live like this. I do, now.

Enjoying the process of shopping for ingredients. Then cooking something lovely.

People who enjoy watching a tv series with their favourite snacks.

That don't see food as simply calories or nutrients.

But an excuse for experiencing great joy.

*Changing your relationship with alcohol, isn't a diet. It's a lifestyle choice. One that holds the potential to transform our life, and even save it.*

Nothing is more important than that.

Wanting to be thin? Wanting to be perfect? It's just another form of looking for approval in all the wrong places, from all the wrong people.

People pleasing is bullshit. Please stop doing it. It only leads you back to the pub. And back to being miserable as ever.

Putting weight on, is a very real fear that I have heard from every single woman, that I've ever helped stop drinking heavily, this way. It's a fear I held too.

I'm not saying it's invalid. Just that its temporary. We can all push through it, to a better place. To real, lasting change, which is our common goal here, let's be honest.

Our physical appearance changes on two levels when we stop drinking.

First of all, our body shape changes, as our hormones finally get to level out after years of being shocked by alcohol.

I changed shape when I stopped drinking. Well, after I was able to drop the disordered eating, anyway. I had curves where curves never existed as a drinker. In fact, my body shape was oddly square, back then.

My face totally changed. I looked decades younger. I still have my actor headshots taken of me aged 22, where I look older than I do now aged 43. Alcohol does weird things to a face. I'm telling you.

Even after having two kids, and a thyroid that no longer works, with the inevitable weight gain that comes as a consequence of both. I still look better than I did as a drinker in my twenties. Maybe not as good as a non-drinker in my thirties, but that's okay. I'll take it!

I don't need other people's approval of my appearance these days, to feel validated. So, I keep loving food, and never revisiting the past nightmares of obsession and restriction, ever again.

These days my face and body reflect a change in my values and my self-esteem, not the consequence of any diet. That's how I maintain my long-lasting change to non-drinker.

The first few weeks of trying to eat like a regular human, is a challenge.

Using the **Shut-Up Alcohol!** tool will help. Because it is still very much the alcohol trying to reassert itself, through calorie controlling. That is the truth of the matter.

Thoughts like; *"I am going to get fat." "Everyone will look at me" "What's the point in all of this if I am not thin.?"* Are all your brain trying to lead you to the familiar pastures of all-or-nothing, thinking.

Which, in turns leads to all the drinking.

It's not worth it.

Be warned. Your brain *will* fight back against those first few **Shut Up, Alcohol!** attempts. It will up the ante *"nobody will find you attractive" "nobody will love you" "you can't expect someone to want to be with a fat non-drinker"* All very charming, totally untrue scripts, straight from my old way of thinking.

Tell them to *shut up*. All those thoughts are wrong. You deserve more. It's time your brain got the memo.

After a few days of really hammering the **Shut Up, Alcohol!** response, causing disruption to these thoughts, and weakening them significantly. Why not take a little break by sitting back and observing them for a while.

Let these stupid notions just run their ridiculous course, as you look on from a distance, like a bystander, listening to the ranting of a nonsensical individual.

It's fascinating, truly. Right up until the point it says something that hits a nerve. Then, you're connecting emotionally with a thought that has the potential to influence you.

That's the best example I can give you, of the optimal point to tell any thought *shut up*.

Okay. So now you've stopped the restrictive eating thought right in its track? Play **The Opposite Game.**

And what does **The Opposite Game** reveal? Probably that we want to feel *accepted, attractive, loved, secure and safe.*

Spoiler alert: none of these things have anything to do with what we look like, in reality.

But until we break the mental association, we have made between them? Eating like a regular human is a challenge. Stick with it though, it's worth it. In fact, everything you really want, lies on the other side of this thought.

Even if you eat everything you want from now until you are an octogenarian, you won't put on piles of weight.

It's not possible once the cycle of drinking and hangovers are broken.

Back when I thought I was restricting my calories, as a heavy drinker. There were the drunken cheesy chips after kicking-out time. The takeaways when I was too fragile to face whatever was going mouldy in my neglected fridge. The hangover fry-ups.

Stopping those food related behaviours, was what really changed how I looked. Well, that and stopping drinking endless pints of lager, obviously.

Start taking an interest in food, instead of seeing it as the enemy. And discover the true joy of what you have been missing out on, for all these years.

Most important of all, It's new. And anything new, automatically has no place in old drinking routines, so by default **must** be building powerful **Non-Drinking**

**Momentum**.

Which is the single most important thing you can be do for yourself, right now.

Adding to the new **Non-Drinking Momentum** snowball, is what's going to maintain our success for years and years and years to come. Both yours and mine.

And it has nothing to do with whether we lose or gain a pound in weight this week.

# CHAPTER 14

# No thanks, I'm not drinking.

"*No thanks, I'm not drinking*"

That's all we need to say, to anyone's offer, anytime, really. This could be the shortest chapter in the history of books.

But of course it's not. And why not?

**Because it's not what we say, it is how we say it**.

People who have always been non-drinkers have no problem telling people that they aren't drinking.

(And whether in the long term, you choose to stop completely, or just drink differently. You will still need to work through the discomfort of turning drinks down without feeling bad about it.)

They won't even point out they're not drinking. Just automatically ask for their usual alcohol-free drink.

It's not a big deal. Nobody cares.

What is really funny is where the attention should actually be in a situation like this.

We've addressed this several times already, but it bears repeating; *chronic drinkers are people pleasers.*

Our bad drunken behaviour invites such disapproval, that we are constantly desperate to make up for it. And we do so by trying to act however other folk need us to, in order for them to think the best of us.

Many have died in their quest to appease other people, through drinking. All in order to make them feel more comfortable. Which is so sad. Let's not do that.

They will never get the golden opportunity that we have right now. To do this wildly differently.

Remember back in the beginning of this book, when I told you about my awful attempt stop drinking in 2004, for those long six weeks, using willpower?

Seared into my mind is the wedding I attended, when the bride and groom both were outraged that I wasn't drinking.

That's how I remember it, anyway.

Were they though? Really? Or did they just object to me hiding in the corner, on the happiest day of their lives. Filtering for everyone else's overflowing glasses of cheer. Wearing a face like a smacked arse.

How did I handle it all at the time? If it was like every other situation in my life, then we can go ahead and assume that the answer is *badly.*

Did I literally refuse to pick up the champagne glass to toast them or something? I honestly can't remember.

Was I feeling self-conscious because I believed everyone was staring at me for not drinking? (How on earth would they know? Demand a swig from my glass presumably. So ridiculous what our minds conjure up sometimes, I swear.)

Was I feeling inadequate because my self-worth came in the currency of being a performing seal, and coming out with drunken quips? This is highly likely.

Shame it would take me years to figure out I'm far funnier as a non-drinker. And no longer ever have to be the butt of anyone's jokes.

How much did my bad attitude itself, draw attention to the fact that I wasn't drinking.

Was it because I was anxious? Was it because I was uncomfortable? Was it because I was not enjoying the situation? Yes.

Was it because I spent the entire time sitting there, building up strong **Drinking Momentum** that I then had to fight against, tooth and nail? Also yes.

How different social occasions are for me these days. I'm so grateful for that.

I love the freedom of them. I truly enjoy naturally gravitating towards people who I know will have great craic.

And I bloody well love that once the problem drinkers start getting drunk, I can take my leave. Whether that's to go to some other nice occasion, or home to my beautiful house.

Because I am not there to be anyone else's drunken entertainment. And neither are you.

No, the special occasions are a doddle, once you get the hang of the **Filtering** exercise we discovered earlier.

It's trying to still hang around with our so-called friends, fellow alcohol abusers, where it all get a bit tricky. And always for the same reason…

My husband loves golf, it's his favourite hobby.

So it stands to reason, that the majority of his friends are golfers. Every single one of those lads love a game of golf.

If they go out after golf, they sit at a table and talk about? You've guessed it; golf.

In their WhatsApp group what are they messaging about? Golf.

*Because that's what happens when you hang around with a load of heavy golfers, right?*

When I was a heavy drinker. All of my friends were very heavy drinkers. What did we talk about? Drinking? What did we plan our social lives around? Bars.

It's all we needed to have in common.

So of course, my so-called friends were outraged when I stopped drinking. I had broken the only rule of our kinship; be a drunken mess.

Think back to anyone in your circle of heavy drinkers, who ever tried to change. And then to the immediate and visceral reaction they were met with.

Let's examine this for what it really is for just a moment...

Back in the day when I was drinking heavily, I needed the people around me, to drink as heavily as me, if not heavier.

Was I using them? Hell yes, I was.

That was not being a real friend in any way, shape, or form to them, clearly, but anyway, moving on.

If anyone tried to challenge that status quo, by attempting to stop drinking or cut down on their drinking? I came down on them like a ton of bricks I'm not proud of that, but it's true.

The objective was to make them feel as uncomfortable as possible, so they would be shamed into getting drunk alongside me. How charming. What a wonderful addition to any friendship group I must have been.

**And all my attitude really achieved, was to point out to everyone within a ten-mile radius, what a chronic problem I had with alcohol.**

If we are indifferent alcohol, can take a drink or leave it just as easily, either way? We would never try to belittle someone for changing such a small part of life as their alcohol consumption.

*And, if you bear that fact in mind from this point onwards? You will never be shamed or intimidated by a person trying to challenge you for ordering a soft drink. Only pity them, whilst sticking to your guns.*

Because their own reaction is giving away what they're trying to keep their most closely guarded secret, even from themselves.

Their reaction is telling the world what a massive problem they have with alcohol.

Their bullying. Their belittling. Even their mere inappropriate questioning, of another person's lifestyle choice. Is showing the world in black-and-white that they are a person with a chronic alcohol abuse issue.

I have nothing but compassion for those sad people, now.

And I thank God I'm not one of them, anymore.

Now we know this secret, it's impossible to feel intimidated by an aggressive, barfly, type of person.

Since we have this new awareness, we won't want to try and people-please them, ever again.

Once we know this, we cannot unknow it. Once we see this, we cannot unsee. The curtain has been pulled back from the mighty Oz.

Normal drinkers may express surprise at our new non-drinking ways. This is understandable. From their vantage point of indifference, they will have been clearly able to see how bad our alcohol abuse was.

Trust me, people quickly forget. They will very swiftly put you in a category of non-drinkers and never think of you as anything but.

There are people in my life that have been there for decades and decades, socially.

Who saw me at my absolute worst. And could easily attest to my ruining many a social occasion, with my terrible drunken behaviour.

Yet they all see me as a non-drinker now. Without any prompting on my part.

Because that's what the human brain does. It takes the current information it's presented with, and it makes it a permanent reality, across all time, past, present, and future.

The only exception to this, is if our attitude when we say we aren't drinking, is super unsure, or apologetic. Because everyone listens to the tone of a person's voice, over the language they are using.

What is your tone actually suggesting? Is it *I'm really sorry but I'm not drinking tonight, what a waste of oxygen I am. Feel free to take the piss out of me mercilessly.*

Is our body language cowering and dejected? If our mannerisms come across as unsure, the barflies will pick us apart in minutes.

Because they will be unsettled now. They have a big question staring them right in the face:

**Will you still be there, if they drink and you don't?**

And you know what? They should be worried. Because the ball is in their court. They now either need to follow our example and face up to their own alcohol issues. Or time to find a new drinking buddy, because we have left the watering hole and we aren't coming back.

We don't have to surround ourselves with people that we don't enjoy spending time with. Non-heavy drinkers know this, but we have to relearn this fact.

Fortunately, most people make it clear whether they are a good match for our new **Non-Drinking Momentum**, very early on.

Sometimes it's uncomfortable. Sometimes it's a relief. And sometimes it's sad. All of its okay. People come and go. The only person we ever have to really live with is ourselves. So let's make us the best person we could ever hope to spend time with!

But what about new friends and acquaintances?

Nobody ever picks up on me being a non-drinker.

My husband and I work together, and a lot of the work that we do takes place in the evening.

We are regularly after dinner speakers at gala events. Unlimited alcohol at every table and well-meaning people always being friendly and trying to fill my glass.

All I have to say is no thank you. No one cares, everyone moves on. It's no different to when I attend them as a guest. To date, no one has demanded I leave and take my pint of fizzy drink with me...

There is no bigger non-drinking incentive, than seeing someone at a very glamorous do they have paid lots of money to attend, being sick all over a banquet table, and ruining any networking opportunities.

Also, riddle me this, has anyone in your entire life ever said the words to you *"which alcoholic beverage would you like?"*

No. Because that person would in fact be an alien. Recently beamed down to earth. Who has learned how to speak, using only the medium of YouTube videos.

Never happens. Its only ever *"what would you like to drink."* Tell them, how simple is that?

These days I am so at peace with my non-drinking, its second nature. I am happy and comfortable with who I am, what I stand for, what my personal preferences, are. So, naturally I am comfortable with the choices and preferences of anyone and everyone who surrounds me. You do what you like, like I'll do as I like. Let's all be happy and enjoy ourselves!

(Except if you are being sick on the table. No more joy for you, good sir.)

I'm not missing out now, but by God, I was missing out before.

Having said all of this, I do want to give you an alternative, particularly if you are in your early days of non-drinking, and working to change things, but have to attend a function that you feel you may not be ready for emotionally, yet.

In which case, I'm a firm believer in telling people exactly what they want or need to hear right now, in order to stop hassling you and leave you alone.

- Tell them you are driving and must have the car first thing tomorrow morning.
- Tell them you are on antibiotics.
- Tell them you developed a sudden allergy to alcohol (It happens more often than you think, I did, but more on that in the Control chapter).

It doesn't matter what the little lie is. Just get them to back off.

The long-term aim is to have a great new life and have people just leave us be in the short-term, so we can get on with it. Until we reach that

wonderful place of confidence. Then you can hit them with your dazzling new non-drinking self, and you won't care a jot for their reaction.

Love me or leave me alone.

Get on board with me, and my fabulous new life, or get lost.

To be successfully indifferent to alcohol is easy in a short amount of time. Developing boundaries and self-respect, are way harder.

# CHAPTER 15

# The other tool you hate.

Much as I favour telling little lies to colleagues, acquaintances, and elderly relatives you don't see very often. I'm less on board with telling porkies to spouses, partners, or people you actually live with.

So much old **Drinking Momentum** is tied up in deceit, it's ideal to get rid of it from any close relationships, in our new way of doing things.

Whether you feel you are authentically a non-drinker, or perhaps a light drinker? Either way, this heavy drinking habit demands a rest. So the first few weeks require no drinking at all.

It's the only way I know to objectively see our old habits in the clearest of lights.

Historically I have had a lot of women say to me that their husband or wife will immediately notice if they stop drinking. And then wanted me to help them come up with a story to tell them.

My reply was always an emphatic *no*. Because they actually won't notice.

Every single person thought I was crazy, obviously. But what would happen after the first session?

They would come back and admit their loved one had not noticed that they'd stopped drinking.

To which I would say, *"erm yeah I know."*

Not as green as I'm cabbage looking, as my nan would say.

Why haven't they noticed? Because they used the second tool that everyone hates, but totally works a treat.

The tool for people not noticing that you're not drinking, is to keep your old drinking routine exactly the same, glass-for-glass.

Buy the same equivalent number of bottles that you always do, just swap them for 0% alcohol content.

Whether it be alcohol-free wine bottles, beer bottles non-alcoholic gin and tonic, any of them, doesn't matter.

The important thing is that you keep consuming your regular amount for the next two weeks.

I appreciate that emotionally, this is hard to do. The latent fear of consuming so-called empty, pointless calories. Not getting any immediate praise by going out of our way and telling anyone, because they are bound to question us and ruin our currently more peaceful home environment.

Challenge those thoughts with the **Opposite Game**. This tool is vital. Every single person sees success with it. It's hard to return to drinking alcohol when you are already far too stuffed with a substitute.

Plus, the amount you have previously been consuming will shock you. It's really hard to drink that amount when you brain is fully switched on. It feels full and uncomfortable, this can only be good.

We want your subconscious mind to accept that the amount you have been normalising for yourself is not remotely physiologically normal. Not at all.

Remember, it's just for two weeks.

After that, we switch it up to more practical long-term drinks and amounts.

I'll admit whilst I do love a mocktail on a night out, at home I shy away from 0% alcohol replacements. The grown-up fizzy drinks or cordials are more my thing. I don't miss alcohol, so I never need to try and mimic the taste of it.

People tend to have a 50-50 split where relationships and alcohol abuse are concerned. Not every heavy drinker is in a relationship with a fellow heavy drinker.

Half the women I have worked with who were in relationships, found me because they were scared to keep drinking in case their partner left them.

The other half? Scared to *stop drinking* in case their partner left them.

At the end of the day, people will do what they want, we cannot make them do anything else. The only person we can masking lasting change for, is ourselves.

Using another person as motivation to stop drinking, is only ever a temporary measure, at best.

A proper, functional, respectful, and loving relationship with ourselves, is the real key to long term non-drinking.

Concentrate on you, and let the cards fall where they may.

That's all a bit wishy-washy and vague though, isn't it? I promised you actual practical stuff, so here goes.

When I was a drinker, I predominantly had relationships with heavy drinkers. None of these relationships were any good, I am equally responsible for that.

As my awareness grew and I struggled with willpower, I would try and find people who could keep me sober. This is not a good reason to be with someone. There needs to be way more compatibility than that.

Again, this never ended well. I would eventually just go off on a bender and they wouldn't see me for days. This was not a nice way to treat anyone. All I can say is I know better now.

When I ventured back into the world, as a non-drinker who was no longer housebound. I naturally gravitated towards non-drinkers, or people who were indifferent to alcohol.

Heavy drinkers, or people with alcohol problems always stayed well-clear of me. We just never seemed to cross paths.

I had been a non-drinker for nine years when I met my husband. Sometimes he drinks. Sometimes he doesn't. It makes no difference to me. It's about the 1000th most interesting thing about him, as far as I am concerned. He is the love of my life and understands me like no one else in the world.

I feel permanently comfortable with him. He always make me feel good about myself. And loves me unconditionally.

This relationship is one I would have been utterly incapable of having, before the journey of becoming a non-drinker, transformed into who I am today.

Basically, what I'm saying is, there's plenty of time ahead. Just work on you and the rest will fall into place without any micro-management.

# CHAPTER 16

# Finances

The trick about successful non-drinking is deciphering which ideas seem like short-term wins but are actually setting us up for long-term failure.

And one of the biggest and best examples of this is our finances.

We've all got years and years' worth of old, unhelpful momentum when it comes to money.

In fact, I would have to say that my financial transformation is the one aspect of my life that's even more dramatic than my non-drinking transformation, even.

Lack mentality abounds, where alcohol abuse exists.

Every heavy drinker I have ever met, has a lack mentality when it comes to money. Because it often directly equates to a lack of alcohol.

Which of course is one of our biggest fears; being without this thing that we feel we need to survive, on so many levels.

Let me tell you about me and my finances when I was a drinker.

Like any teenager, money was in short supply. And so I would gravitate towards cheap booze to get my money's worth.

From there, it was off to Uni. Where money was still tight on the ground.

I graduated and was never particularly successful in work. Then constantly drunk, so no real earning potential there. Off back to drama school where I earned my money working in a bar, so you can guess how effective that was.

As an actor-in-residence I earned a pittance. Which takes me up to being housebound for three years and having to declare bankruptcy.

All in all, very little money came into my experience.

This wasn't all bad.

*Because having money was dangerous for me.*

To have money was to be able to drink as much as I could physically get my hands on, which never ended well.

So, the struggle for money was, in a way, how I kept myself safe. Being broke was the only form of self-care I really knew. It meant that often, there was only just enough to drink amounts that wouldn't hurt me too badly. A sort of reprieve.

I wasn't a capable adult. I did not pay my bills on time.

I felt completely powerless when it came to my finances.

So the idea of using sobriety as a form of money-saving, was very tempting.

Except that unfortunately, like everything in my willpower method, it kept leading me right back to drinking,

Because that lack mentality contains so much old **Drinking Momentum**, the struggle is too much to overcome.

I spend way more money as a non-drinker than I ever did as a drinker.

Because I earn way more money as a non-drinker than I ever did as a drinker.

I love earning money and I equally love spending money. Where once I resented every penny that left my bank account that didn't go straight on alcohol, I now love paying people.

Because the feelings of energy exchange and connection that take place through joyfully paying others. Are the polar opposite of the loneliness of heavy drinking.

The kind of which I had never experienced before I shifted my *lack* beliefs into *have* beliefs.

A lot of us are in financial dire straits when we stop drinking, and that can be a trigger to start drinking again. Because we're facing up to the mess that would be easier to stick our heads in the sand about.

But what is the real cost of going back to drinking? The toll on our mental and physical health. The opportunities we squander. The experiences we miss out on.

And what about the priceless things? What might you be sacrificing by continuing to drink today, that cannot be bought? Time. That's the most obvious one.

Nobody can buy time. Even the richest person in the world cannot buy their time back.

It is the real luxury item So, how do we get as much time as possible?

*By allowing ourselves to be present every single second of the day and seeing that for the gift it is. Not a punishment that must be endured.*

And how do we then learn to enjoy this ability to be fully present every single moment? Investing in ourselves, for once.

Spending money in ways we never would have dreamed of doing before. Big or small. Whatever fits our current budget. Anything is better than pouring money down our throats anymore.

Isn't it funny how as heavy drinkers, everything in the world seems like a waste of money, except something that will get us drunk? That never seems like a frivolity, does it?

The more I overcame this belief, and continued to invest in myself, the more I shored up this version of me that would never put up with the treating myself like trash, ever again.

It's a win-win to only have the best.

If you find yourself trying to save money, just in case you might need to squander it down the road on a heavy drinking session. Get ahead of yourself and spend it on something that celebrates this wonderful new life you are building.

# CHAPTER 17

# Certainty

There are many geniuses throughout the decades, who have written beautifully about alcohol-free living.

People who set up fantastic forums. Invented brilliant addiction therapies.

Every single book and method is important and needed by someone. Some are lauded worldwide, others by a handful of grateful followers.

There is only one area of non-drinking, in which I am totally unparalleled.

**I am rock solid in my certainty.**

I am 100% certain.

I am a deliberate non-drinker.

Utterly and powerfully indifferent to alcohol.

Unshakably so.

I was able to create this unbreakable amount of certainty, from a background of formerly being chronically uncertain about everything. That still astounds me, to this very day.

I have never met anyone more certain about their actions when it comes to nondrinking, than I am.

And I can only think that it is to do with the circumstances in which I devised the system.

And the very dramatic, indeed quite traumatic, life lessons during that time.

I know how to be deliberately certain.

I know how to maintain and build on that certainty.

And I know how to teach it effectively too.

The support I feel from the **Non-Drinking Momentum** I have built over the years, now carries me effortlessly through life.

But support is not even a strong enough word for it. Because it is so apparent, it is almost tactile. So real to me, it's like feeling the support of an entire army around me, wherever I go and whatever I do.

I never second-guess my choices. Non-drinking or otherwise. My mind is decisive or peaceful. No going backwards and forwards over the same old things.

I permanently feel in the right place at the right time. After years of feeling so chronically awkward and uncomfortable, I would often check to see if I had put my shoes on the wrong feet or had my clothes on inside out, (which I often did, because hello hangover) everything feels right.

Gone are the days of feeling vulnerable to external circumstances.

Of feeling so powerless in every single situation, that I didn't know there was any other way to feel.

Now I feel positively *charged* with empowerment, in every single moment of every single day.

I expect to go about my days feeling inspired, uplifted, certain and solid.

It's like drinking me, was made of paper, and non-drinking me, was forged out of steel.

What a sacrifice it would be to give up living this way!

If I had to go back to being drunk tomorrow, I don't think I could cope.

But to go back to the chronic uncertainty that went along with the drinking, would be worse than going back to the drinking itself.

I'm totally indifferent alcohol. I really don't care about it at all.

But if you asked me to give up my constant sense of certainty, I don't know how I would survive.

Practising certainty is the biggest sense of relief it is possible to feel. And if you practise the sentences below, you will cultivate a sense of certainty so fast, you will be wondering where the hell it has been all your life.

**I am sure.**

**I am solid.**

**I am certain.**

**I am good.**

**I know.**

**I've got this.**

**This is who I really am.**

**I am building an incredible new life.**

**This is all so easy.**

**I am the person to please.**

**I have always been a non-drinker.**

**I deserve the best of all things**.

Say these sentences after you do a **Shut Up, Alcohol!** to counteract any niggles of uncertainty when they arise?

And I assure you, there is no environment you will be tempted in.

There is not a relationship that will pull you off course.

Because, with certainty. You. Just. Know. Always.

# CHAPTER 18

# Creativity

I'm going to be honest and admit that in my very early days I would have had no time for this concept.

But the truth is that every single authentic non-drinker who is still drinking, has a lack of creative outlet. Which is something we all actually need to cultivate, in order to be successful non-drinkers.

I never thought of myself as a creative individual. Unless creating drunken drama and chaos counts, in which case I was basically Van Gogh.

In fact, regularly I would refer to myself as somebody with not a creative bone in her body.

Not a nice thing to say about myself. But most of the stuff I said about myself back then wasn't very nice, obviously.

Because all heavy drinkers have low self-esteem.

You don't hurt yourself and like yourself at the same time, it's not possible.

Creative outlets shore up long-term, effortless non-drinking success.

Every single one of us is naturally creative.

Have you ever met a child that did not have an innate sense of creativity?

Of course not, we are all natural born creators.

As soon as we start drinking heavily and that becomes our default hobby or defining characteristic though?

There is no room for creativity.

We don't just freeze our development into adults and responsible individuals.

We stop our creativity.

One of the biggest misnomers of the past, that is thankfully now seen as outdated, was the concept of the tortured soul who needed alcohol to create great works of genius.

Any success these individuals had were in spite of the fact that they drank a lot. Not because of it.

And of course all future works of greatness were cut short if they died of alcoholism.

Can't argue with that.

Sadly, it takes a very determined person to create in spite of alcoholism or addiction.

Those of us who choose to stop drinking and keep doing it? To maintain our success as non-drinkers, we must tap back into our natural born creativity, that has been left unused for so long.

We must find it. And then find it anew, because it changes as often as a new strong personal preference, evolves within us.

Often it is easiest to start with something that will impact us positively and immediately.

Turning one of our stumbling blocks into an outlet for creativity is a huge win.

Let's take our home environment, for example. Most of us only start to truly take in our surroundings when we stop drinking.

Unfortunately, it is the exception to the rule when people find themselves living in surroundings that place them.

However, some people do become fixated on maintaining a façade to hide their chaotic drinking, and their homes are an immaculate nod to their notions of perfection. Perpetuating the myth, so they can be left alone to drink without intervention.

So it's not to say that everyone is like me, who lived in really horrible surroundings. With no care or clue, of how to change it.

But some are. And we wake up to our surroundings, realising the awful living environment looks exactly how we have felt on the inside, for years.

Which gives us a lovely opportunity to flex our creative muscles for the first time, to change all of that.

For many reasons, our home can be a major bug bear in those early days, weeks, and months.

So getting creative with our actual living space, proves to us that we are capable of change. It's also useful to form new routines, whilst working out strong personal preferences.

Not to mention, it's a lot easier to stay away from the pub, if we have somewhere nicer to be.

Moving on from there, some people find joy in exploring activities they did when they were young, whether it be a sport, or musical instrument.

After my sorry attempts at Yoga, it turned out, that I really liked Pilates. Then there was colouring in, which I still love to do to this day.

I love to watch television. You say that to a person who has never had an alcohol problem and they won't get it at all. But I was never able to immerse myself in watching anything, back in my drinking days.

Now books and television are such a nice way to dreamily lose track of time, it's a lovely experience.

I love crafting. That's been my most recent joyful discovery. Who knew?! It's astonishing, the things we discover about our real selves.

A lot of people who stop drinking, or drastically change their relationship with alcohol, and get creative, turn their hobbies into side businesses. Some even go one step further and turn that side business into a full-time career. It is such an exciting evolution to witness.

A journey so far-removed from the sterile, sober-and-perfect attempts of using willpower. It's not even in the same stratosphere.

# CHAPTER 19

# Why it's not about how much we drink.

I mentioned earlier that I used to talk on and radio and write in various online publications about my alcohol-free life.

Until I got discouraged and stopping do all of it, altogether.

A lot of it was due to the same irritating question about how much I used to drink.

This question alienates more problem drinkers, than any other.

The more we choose to obsess on the amount of drinking other people do, the more likely we are to keep justifying our own drinking.

What do I mean by that?

Well, it doesn't matter how much I drank. And it doesn't matter how much you drink.

It doesn't matter how much the person next to you us drinks.

Unless the person asking you this question is a doctor, there is absolutely no relevance.

**It's not about how much you drink, it's about how much what you are drinking affects you.**

Some people can put away a shockingly tremendous amount of alcohol. Yet not really suffer too many immediate physical or psychological ramifications.

No black outs. Job losses. No stays in hospital.

Yet.

But if I had waited until my drinking levels matched absolutely every hardened drinker I had ever met, I'd have died instead of creating a new life for myself.

I'll say it again,

It's nothing to do with the amount we drink. It's about how much the amount we drink, affects us.

Affects our day-to-day living of life.

Affects our important relationships.

Affects our finances.

Don't ever wait for that magic number. Don't ever wait for the amount that will suddenly make you go *"oh yeah me too, gosh. I'll stop drinking now."* Because that day will never arrive,

You will always find a way to persuade yourself otherwise.

The last few years of my drinking, I always found a way of using someone in recovery's "Before story", to convince myself I was fine.

Either they drank a lot more than me so wasn't relevant.

Or they didn't drink enough for me, and I'd look down my nose at them for being hysterical.

I would think of them as the white wine spritzer brigade.

The "mummy needs wine" drinkers, who I judged terribly and never took their plight seriously. Because I was arrogant and knew nothing.

Alcohol units are not an accurate enough yardstick to measure problem drinking.

There are other, far more important amounts to be concentrating on.

How often is my mind free from alcohol-related thoughts? How many things do I do that never involve drinking?

How many days have I called in to work sick with a hangover this year, so far?

How much happiness do I genuinely feel?

What amount of people are there in my life, that care for me and truly like me for who I am?

Those are the amounts that we want to concentrate on.

The amount that I'm getting to evolve as a person.

The amount of experiences I get to have.

The amount of meaningful exchanges with other people.

The amount of memories made, and experiences had..

Here are the big ones: **what's the amount of certainty that I'm feeling about me/my life/myself, right now. What amount of love am I able to feel for myself, and other people**.

Those are the only measuring units I give a shit about, quite frankly.

# CHAPTER 20

# Controlling Alcohol

This is the chapter that I never thought I'd write. It's certainly not what I originally designed this method for.

I designed **Shut Up, Alcohol!** as a method to stop myself drinking.

And it worked.

As I mentioned earlier, when you put something out there in the public domain, teaching it to other people, it's going to evolve and get bigger than you thought.

I've already told you the story about that the first lady that came to me and said that she'd failed, and was really upset about it.

It's these sorts of experiences that make me feel ambivalent towards sober cliques.

I cannot stand the thought of anyone being forced into isolation, because the way they choose to change their lives, isn't a way others approve of.

Drinking a little bit of alcohol has never been something that I've ever had aspirations of doing.

Alcohol holds no attraction for me. My life was crap when I drank it. And now I don't drink it, my life is spectacular. But I went through a proper journey of discovery to find out that this is who I really am. And there's power in that.

*I am not missing out now, I was missing out, back then.* But not everyone feels this way.

And to be of service to as many people, unnecessarily struggling with alcohol, as possible, I have to understand where they are coming from.

I have heard from a great deal of people over this past decade, who discovered that their core selves, were light drinkers. And they used my method to become indifferent to alcohol. which provided them with real freedom.

We have already established that none of us are authentic heavy drinkers. Or we would never be interested in drinking a different way. So let's cross that possibility off the list.

To me, the two options left are:

- Effortlessly teetotal.
- Effortlessly light drinker.

*The effortless aspect makes them both feel almost identical, in practise. So the only way to know which is the true you, is to identify which gives you the biggest feeling of peace. Of feeling right. In the flow of things. That's how nondrinking felt for me, as soon as I started supporting myself with the tools in this book.*

And because it felt so right? I never explored the other option. Much like when I met my husband I didn't have to date anyone else ever again, just to make sure he was the one. He just is. So that was it for me where dating was concerned.

But I have been doing this method with other people, for long enough to know when they are faking it to achieve perfection. And that's not *the point. The point is empowering self-discovery. Otherwise there can be no true closure and resolution where heavy drinking is concerned.*

So, if you have nailed the rest of my method, done all of the homework in the order of, and duration that I requested. But still feel like you haven't connected with your authentic self? Okay, fair enough, read on.

### *But please do not read the rest of this chapter if:*

- Your doctor has told you that you will die if you continue to drink any amount of alcohol.
- You have been charged with, or have a history of, drink-driving.
- You are currently achieving sobriety using the Alcoholics Anonymous 12 step method.
- You have ever been hospitalised with serious drinking related injuries.
- You have ever lost custody of your children.

None of what I am about to discuss is appropriate for you. Please stick with what has worked for you in the past and keep up the amazing work.

Anyone else, feel free to read on, and keep an open mind…

After I realised that some women were successfully drinking moderate amounts, and going to great lengths to hide it, I realised to keep them safe, we had to invent strict rules.

The rules had to be strict at first, because **No Manual**. It takes practice to become who we really are. A lot of undoing old unhelpful habits. This can only happen in a place that feels supportive and safe.

So, after some trial and error, our safety and support rules, boiled down to these:

- No more than three alcoholic drinks in an evening.
- No day drinking, under any circumstances.

- Every alcoholic drink consumed had to be interspersed with a non-alcoholic drink in between them all.

- The alcoholic drink of choice could not be a neat spirit.

- Nor could it be a former go-to drink from back in heavy drinking days.

- The three-drink maximum could not be utilised every time they drank.

And if they tried to bend any of these rules, it was back to the drawing board.

*The idea behind my method is that alcohol does not take up space in our lives, or thoughts, anymore.*

That's how we become indifferent to it, and it no longer holds any power over us.

So, even as occasional drinkers, new **Non-Drinking Momentum** had to be built. There was to be no sliding back into a life where alcohol took the centre stage.

I already knew that drinking small amounts was no guarantee that a person didn't have an alcohol problem.

I discovered this, not through personal experience, as we all know by now, I was a thirsty drinker, and no mistake.

No, it was through working with a lady who anybody would classify as a light drinker.

I could not understand why she had found me at all. But it soon became clear that her drinking was actually ruling her life.

She did drank every night without fail, which is not something I would ever recommend.

But the amount she was drinking was so small, it seemed negligible, on the surface.

Nevertheless, hers was one of the most restrictive and narrow lives I've ever seen, and it was so sad.

Every night at 6pm on the dot, she would pour herself a tiny glass of red wine and start to take miniscule sips.

It would take her the entire evening to finish two small glasses. But finish them she would.

She invented this ritual because, having witnessed so much addiction in her formative years, she didn't want to become like many other family members.

Drinking thoughts totally ruled her life.

As soon as she woke in the morning, she would remind herself how many hours were to go before she could have her glasses of wine.

All day at work it would be at the front of her thoughts.

She wouldn't go and see her children or grandchildren.

Every night she would race straight home to make sure she had her first glass sat in front of her at 6pm.

She never went away on holiday.

Never did she go out for dinner.

Her kids and grandkids never saw her, unless they agreed to only come around on a weekend morning.

Her life consisted of her ritual, and that was it. Alcohol had been elevated to such a high place for her, she couldn't have prioritised it more if she tried

And nobody took her problem seriously. Imagine even trying to go to rehab for two small glasses of wine a night? She would have been laughed out of the waiting room.

It really was one of the toughest situations I've ever seen.

This habit have been ingrained in her for decades and decades and decades.

And really, there was no physical need to stop, she wasn't endangering herself massively.

She was just obsessed. It was completely ruining her life and leaving her lonely.

I am so pleased to say that she now does not drink at all! She has a fully rounded life, and alcohol plays no part in it. All through doing the exercises on herself that you've already read through. Incorporating them into her daily life and, most importantly, understanding the accidental **Drinking Momentum** she was unwittingly building so strongly.

I'm so proud of the amazing changes she has made to her own life.

I say this to you not because I want to control how you use this method. I genuinely don't.

I just want you to be aware that you can drink very small amounts, especially compared to how much you have consumed in the past.

And still be making drinking your number one priority. Instead of living a great, restriction-free life. And there's nothing authentically living about that.

The thing is, I worried about these women who said they were successfully controlling alcohol and had found their true peace as lighter drinkers.

Were they honestly following the strict framework that we had designed together for them?

They seemed happy and relieved to be living their truth, instead of lying to please me, or be seen as perfect.

But was it real?

Just because I knew everything that I had ever read or heard about willpower method, to be false for me, didn't mean Moderation Management wasn't dangerous.

In fact, the late inventor of this phrase, and movement, realised she couldn't drink that way after all. And ended up re-joining Alcoholics Anonymous. Which always sent huge alarm bells sounding for me.

Was I being incredibly naïve? Could I be 100% sure that the former heavy drinkers, using my method, weren't just all in denial and putting on a front?

I couldn't ever really say for sure, either way. So when it came to writing about them, and their rules, in this book?

I found I couldn't do it.

**Everything I have ever taught has always come from a place of real-life experience.**

**I've never taken anyone else's word for anything. Second hand ideas and experiences are not powerful or reliable enough for me. I have to live through and fully immerse myself in a situation, or it holds no personal value.**

I am many things, but never a hypocrite.

The way I saw it, I had two choices:

- Pretend these women and their experiences didn't exist and write a nice little book on total abstinence, which is how I do live my life, but not how they truthfully live theirs. Totally ignoring how
- integral our authentic core preferences are for indifference to alcohol.
- Try their strict framework for myself and see if it really did work like they claimed.

**And that Dear Reader, was how, at the end of 2021, I started drinking again.**

Well for a few months, anyway.

I didn't discuss why I was doing it, with anyone.

Not even my husband. Whom I tell every thought to, *loudly*, pretty much the moment it enters my head. Whether he needs to hear it or not.

(A character trait which makes me an absolute *joy* to watch any Netflix series with, as you can imagine.)

I was aware it sounded crazy. So, I just didn't give my reasons.

A month or two before I recommenced drinking. I started dropping it casually into conversations. Luckily it was lockdown, so most people were also going stir crazy and saying ridiculous things.

At first, Mr C. assumed I was joking, but eventually he realised I wasn't. Fortunately, he is the most laid-back person I have ever known (when it comes to anything that isn't a competition). So, he just let me go on with my musings, unchallenged.

Waiting a few months was the first test I set myself. An opportunity to fall at the first hurdle, if you will.

If I made the decision to start drinking, then immediately sprinted to nearest off-licence, waving my bottle opener in the air like a flare gun? Then that's a fairly good indicator drinking was going to turn ugly for me, really fast.

No urge followed my decision. I waited, then waited some more. But nothing

Eventually I decided to do it. My husband took me for dinner at his golf club, and I felt like it was as good a time as any, to get my drink on.

Following the strict framework my ladies claimed to still be using. I knew lager was out of the question. Seeing as it had been my drink of choice for years.

Instead, I went for a drink I had never tried, but had become so popular in the last few years, even I remembered its name: Prosecco.

The way this drink was talked about, I thought it had to be the best tasting thing on the planet. Why else would its name be glorified all over cushions notebooks, pink t-shirts, and have full bottomless brunches given in its honour?

I took my first sip, and can I just say, ladies, *what the hell are you people thinking?*

Though I have never actually imbibed a glass of cat urine. Prosecco is the closest I will hopefully ever come to trying.

It smelled foul and tasted worse. Never mind any underlying fear of being unable to stop myself going on a mad sesh, it was all I could do to get a few sips down my neck.

A far cry from the days of drinking so many pints of lager a night, I may as well have had my bar stool set up in the loos…

The same thing happened with every alcoholic drink I tried over the next few months. Every single one tasted rank. Made me feel tired. And I had to brush my teeth half a dozen times to get rid of the aftertaste.

Regularly I found myself doing the very action that had always been shrouded in mystery to me, when I was a heavy drinker.

Yes, I became one of those weirdos who **forget that they have a drink on the go**. Actually *leaving a half-drunk glass on the table* to go warm/flat/wasted.

The one thing I *cannot* honestly claim, is if I would have stopped trying to drink under my own steam.

I had a plan to try it for six months because this seemed like a thorough enough amount of time.

I was even hoping to get electrodes attached to my head, to see if my brain was reacting to the alcohol physiologically, despite me being emotionally indifferent to it. *Because science.*

But lockdown wouldn't have made that possible, and anyway, three months in, I tried a glass of champagne and had an allergic reaction to it.

Can you imagine that?! What I wouldn't have given for such a thing to happen when I was desperate to stop drinking in 2004!

Though in all honestly it wouldn't have stopped me. Only added to my drinking related injuries.

After the allergic reaction, I was done with drinking. And it was a massive relief for many reasons.

- The women who claimed to be drinking small amounts without any impact on their lives anymore, were clearly telling the truth.
- I was definitely an authentic non-drinker after all.
- Building strong **Non-Drinking Momentum** works for people who want to deliberately control their alcohol intake, as long as they keep doing the homework.

One thing I will say is that even the tiny amounts I was drinking, slowed me down. I wasn't as interested in my hobbies, or the wider world around me. So, even though I wasn't invested in it, the small introduction of alcohol back into my life, had made my world and my interests, a bit narrower, (though like I say, it was lockdown so even that's not an absolute truth I can 100% attest to.)

My mood was lower. I was not as cynical as I had been, back in my bad old days of drinking. But I was not as naturally bright as my default setting is these days.

(Why did I just describe myself as an iPhone, not a person? Don't worry we are nearly at the end; I surely cannot fit in many more terrible analogies.)

In all good conscience, I can still only tell you what I personally have experienced, which is, if you follow my method to the letter, then after 15 years of effortless non-drinking, you may get the same results as me, if you choose to reintroduce alcohol into the equation.

Either way, please don't bend or break the rules, they were designed to make us indifferent to alcohol. And without indifference, we are just pretending to find this journey effortless.

If you do find yourself diving back into heavy drinking? Stop and seek help immediately. It could very well save your life.

# CHAPTER 21

# Biscuits

I was raised Roman Catholic. When I was in primary school, the priests and nuns were still responsible for our religious instruction, if not much of our formal education.

We would learn from them the Ten Commandments. Stations of the Cross. Meaning of Advent. They would give us bible lessons, stain of original sin, eternal damnation etc. You know, all the good stuff.

And it was in one of these lessons that my first major spiritual quandary, occurred.

My birthday fell during Lent!

Poor Jesus fasted forty days and forty nights, (not sure why the latter part is always stated, surely, it's a given? It's not like he prayed, starved, and renounced the devil during the day, only to sneak off down the Bigg Market by nightfall.) to save mine and my tiny schoolmate's tiny, immortal souls.

But could I really give up chocolate for him? For forty whole days (and forty nights, obvs.)

No. I could not.

What's a lass to do? Cake, whilst a rare treat, was not a safe option, who wants a Lent birthday without cake?!

No, my sacrifice would have to be something I wouldn't mind forgoing on my Big Day. Something I was indifferent to.

Biscuits. I just wasn't bothered by them. I only ever really had them when visiting grandparents, who would of course, congratulate me on my sacrifice, and maybe even give me 50p for my trouble!

It was the perfect solution.

I started giving up biscuits for Lent in the 1980's, and still do so today.

Can you guess what happened?

Forty days (and forty nights) of being annually biscuit-less, have resulted in biscuits taking pride of place, 325 days a year.

I love them. My biscuit tin is always fully stocked. Never do I leave a supermarket without at least one packet of biscuits in my trolley.

It is safe to say that over four decades, I have elevated biscuits to a place they do not belong.

And that, had I not chosen to complicate my relationship with biscuits, from such a young age, I would have spent my entire life being indifferent to them.

If I were to stop participating in Lent, biscuits would no doubt fade into the background.

But it's a ritual that's still very important to me, for many reasons. It connects me to my past. Serves as a reminder of who I am, and where I came from. Two things that I don't ever want to lose sight of. No matter how far removed my day-to-day life is from it all, now.

And so. I will keep elevating those sweet little snacks, to a place they have no business being, in mine or anyone else's life.

*But if they ever started making my world as small a place as alcohol once did?*

*And if they became the thing I lived for, rather than just a slightly odd fixation? Then that would be time for a major re-think…*

# CHAPTER 22

# Before you go...

(I can't believe we are at the end of the book already! Where does the time go, eh?

There's a few things that are important to know, but not long enough to have a chapter of their own, so I'm sticking 'em down here, have a read and then we shall say our goodbyes...)

I've already mentioned that counting days is, as far as I am concerned, for people in prison. I can understand why they do it. For them, it's a countdown to better beginnings.

But our bright future has already begun.

Accountability is a tool a lot of people swear by. I don't feel it's massively effective myself. I broke every sober promise that I ever made myself, before inventing **Shut Up, Alcohol!** My own vows and words were empty and meaningless.

In fact, I actually spent so much time and effort trying to find holes and clauses in my own contracts, that it consumed me. So important was it that I be seen to be keeping my own word, that I would try and use the most ridiculous and delusional excuses to start drinking again.

No one cared, I was the only one participating in this ridiculous charade, everyone else was busy having a proper life.

Count days if you must, just bear in mind people who use this tool have an 85% failure rate of getting to one year sober, and a 95% failure after that.

Not the sort of odds I find reassuring...

Instead, why not count the width of your light/non-drinking? The number of new things you have tried? New places you have been? New experiences undertaken?

How many new friends made. Hobbies you've given a whirl? New skills learned.

That's the sort of counting that really does work. I use it myself all of the time, even after 17 years (in 2023) of being indifferent to alcohol.

A wide life is a full life, is a good life. Just a little something to think about!

Something else to bear in mind, is that values are a wonderful thing, that become instantly useless, the moment they are forced upon another person... Everyone deserves to feel valid and respected, whether we agree with their way of doing things, or not. Our way of building a new life is just that, our way.

Methods are not contagious. You won't catch A.A. from standing too near someone who follows the 12-step method. Let them live their life as freely as you wish to live yours. The stronger your personal preferences get, the more confident and peaceful you will be in the company of people, who approach drinking in a different way to you.

You may not ever be able to make them feel the same way back, but that's okay. You can only be responsible for your own choices. Don't ever apologise for that.

Life is not a competition. Please don't tell my husband I said that.

I hope you have enjoyed my little book that only took an entire decade of my life to finish.

Hopefully you have discovered a few new tools to help you on your way to a fabulous life, free of **Drinking Momentum**.

There are so many more tools that I have added along the way. But I wanted to only include the easiest ones that everyone has always grasped quickly and that had the most effect.

If you want the secret chapter that I didn't include in this little book, feel free to message me asking for it, on Twitter/X, LinkedIn, or Instagram, where I have joint accounts with my husband, @ClarkeandCarrie Carlisle, and I will send it to you!

If you want any more confirmation to prove I am a real human who lives happily as a non-drinker in the real world. Come and see our work at www.clarkeandcarrie.com

Keep building the strong, deliberate, and powerful **Non-Drinking Momentum**. No matter which path you choose. You've got this. I'm so proud of you.

Carrie x

Printed in Great Britain
by Amazon

27827948R00076